BY
DANIEL COYLE

THE
CULTURE PLAYBOOK

THE CULTURE PLAYBOOK

60 HIGHLY EFFECTIVE

ACTIONS TO HELP

YOUR GROUP SUCCEED

DANIEL COYLE

BANTAM BOOKS • NEW YORK

Published in the United States by Bantam Books,
an imprint of Random House,
a division of Penguin Random House LLC, New York.

BANTAM BOOKS and the HOUSE colophon are registered trademarks of
Penguin Random House LLC.

LIBRARY OF CONGRESS CATALOGING-IN-PUBLICATION DATA
Names: Coyle, Daniel, author.
Title: The culture playbook : 60 highly effective actions to
help your group succeed / Daniel Coyle.
Description: New York : Random House, [2022]
Identifiers: LCCN 2021054654 (print) | LCCN 2021054655 (ebook) |
ISBN 9780525620730 (hardcover) | ISBN 9780525620747 (ebook)
Subjects: LCSH: Teams in the workplace. | Corporate culture. | Leadership.
Classification: LCC HD66 .C676 2022 (print) | LCC HD66 (ebook) |
DDC 658.4/022—dc23/eng/20211227
LC record available at https://lccn.loc.gov/2021054654
LC ebook record available at https://lccn.loc.gov/2021054655

International edition ISBN 978-0-593-50091-0

Printed in Canada on acid-free paper

randomhousebooks.com

987654321

FIRST EDITION

Book design by Barbara M. Bachman
Illustrations by Mike Rohde, assisted by Zoe Coyle

For Jenny

CONTENTS

INTRODUCTION

WHERE DOES GREAT CULTURE COME FROM? HOW DO you get it, or turn around a culture that needs fixing?

Most people believe that culture is determined by your group's identity—by who you are. Strong, established cultures like Disney, Apple, and the U.S. Marine Corps feel so special and distinctive that they seem almost predestined. In this way of thinking, a group's culture is a fixed quality, rooted deep within its DNA. Certain special groups possess the gift of great culture; others don't.

I'd like to argue for a different idea:

Your Culture = Your Actions

I believe culture doesn't depend on who you are but on what you do. Culture is not a gift you receive; it's a skill you learn. And like any skill, it can be done well or poorly.

You've likely experienced both good and bad cultures. You know the warm, energizing cohesion of strong culture, the chilly dysfunction of weak culture, and the lurching roller coaster of the places in between. What you might not know, however, is how much power you have to control, strengthen, and transform your group's culture—if you take the right actions.

I've spent the past decade studying some of the most successful, cohesive cultures on the planet—including the U.S. Women's National Soccer Team, Pixar, IDEO, the San Antonio Spurs, and others. In 2018, I wrote *The Culture Code*, which explored the science of building great culture—and which propelled me further into that world. I've consulted with businesses, professional sports teams, and the military, as well as top-performing groups in education, technology, and the not-for-profit sector. I've gone behind the scenes and studied what works, what doesn't, and why.

Early in my journey, I began capturing and analyzing the regimen of actions great groups use to build and sustain their cultures. Every time I encountered a useful method—a cohesion-building technique, a connective habit, a chemistry-igniting tip—I jotted it down and tucked it away in a file I titled "Good Stuff." As time went by, the file kept growing—and growing. Eventually it grew big enough that I felt compelled to assemble the tips into a useful, shareable form. To create a catalog of field-tested culture-building actions—a playbook.

THE
CULTURE PLAYBOOK

RULES FOR
USING THIS BOOK

Rule 1:
Start Where You're At

IT'S TEMPTING TO ASSUME that great cultures exist on a higher plane, in a happy, friction-free world where problems and disagreements happen rarely, and that everything they touch turns to gold. Let me emphasize: *This is not true.* Strong cultures wrestle with plenty of problems, disagree vigorously, and fail with regularity. The difference is, strong cultures experience these problems, disagreements, and failures within bonds of strong, secure connection, and they use them as leverage to learn and improve. (See Tip #23: Kill the Happy Smoothness Fallacy.) So don't start out chasing a tension-free fantasy, because that will only lead to frustration. Instead, take a skills-based approach. Begin by reflecting on where your group is strong and where it's weak. Are you good at creating belonging, but do you struggle with creating purpose? Are you skilled at sharing risk, but less so at giving everyone a strong sense of connection? Start by building on your strengths; then address your weaknesses.

It's also important to keep in mind that while these tips are meant to apply to everyone, bias and unfairness can be baked into institutions and processes in a variety of insidious ways—so it's crucial to keep diversity, equality, and inclusion at the fore when implementing any of these actions.

Rule 2:
Create Conversations, Not Mandates

SOME OF YOU, PARTICULARLY leaders, may be tempted to use these tips to construct a top-down culture-improvement program for your group. Resist this temptation. Groups don't improve their culture by mere compliance; rather, they co-create a shared path and navigate it together. Use the actions that follow to generate reflection and conversation, and see where they lead you. To that end, I've included a handful of activities and exercises to help you assess your group's culture, build your game plan, and track your progress.

Rule 3:
There Are No Rules

DON'T THINK OF THIS book as a rigid blueprint to be followed; rather, think of it as a set of proven actions that can still be improved. Test, tweak, and customize these actions to your group's individual needs. Figure out what works for you, and don't sweat the rest. Culture is always changing and evolving; your job is to continually adapt, respond, and perform the actions that keep it strong and healthy.

Most of all, let go of the outdated belief that great culture is reserved only for certain groups. Culture is not magic, and it's never written in stone. Your group's culture consists of living relationships working toward a shared goal, and it's built by the actions you take together, starting now.

**BUILDING
SAFETY**

**SHARING
VULNERABILITY**

**ESTABLISHING
PURPOSE**

THE STRUCTURE
OF SUCCESS

—

YOU MIGHT BE STARTING OUT THINKING, AS MANY PEOPLE do, that culture is "the soft stuff"—the warm and fuzzy intangibles. In fact, nothing could be further from the truth. Science has shown that strong culture is created by the continual exchange of three key behaviors, which form the sections of this book and also give us our starting point to begin building your group's game plan.

BUILDING YOUR GAME PLAN:

STEP ONE

————

LET'S START BY DEFINING YOUR GROUP. WRITE DOWN the name of a team you're part of, the one you work with most often, whose success is interdependent with yours. Tip: Think smaller rather than larger.

The name of our group is

_____

Our main job is to

_____

_____

How strong is your group's culture right now? Not how strong you wish it were, but how strong it really is. Shade in each of the measures below, from 1 (low) to 5 (high).

SAFETY

LOW ☐☐☐☐☐ HIGH

1 = No one feels connected →→→ 5 = Everyone shares a strong sense of belonging

How does this show itself in your group?

VULNERABILITY

LOW ☐☐☐☐☐ HIGH

1 = Everyone keeps to themselves →→→ 5 = We trust
and share everything, no matter how hard

How does this show itself in your group?

_____

_____

_____

_____

_____

_____

YOUR TURN

PURPOSE

LOW ☐☐☐☐☐ HIGH

1 = We lack direction →→→ 5 = We move urgently toward a larger, shared goal

How does this show itself in your group?

_____

_____

_____

_____

_____

_____

Now let's look closer:

> What does our group look like at our very best?
> Describe the behaviors and activities that generate
> the most energy, connection, and sense of shared
> purpose. (It might help to imagine being visited by a
> documentary film crew—what would they witness?)

_____

_____

_____

_____

YOUR TURN

> What factors stop us from being at our best all
> the time? Name the specific barriers—habits,
> constraints, traditional ways of doing things—
> that stand in your way.
>
> Barrier #1

_____

Barrier #2

_____

Barrier #3

_____

What about our culture is so central and fundamental
that we should never change it?

_____

_____

_____

_____

If we could change one thing about our culture,
what would it be?

_____

_____

_____

YOUR TURN

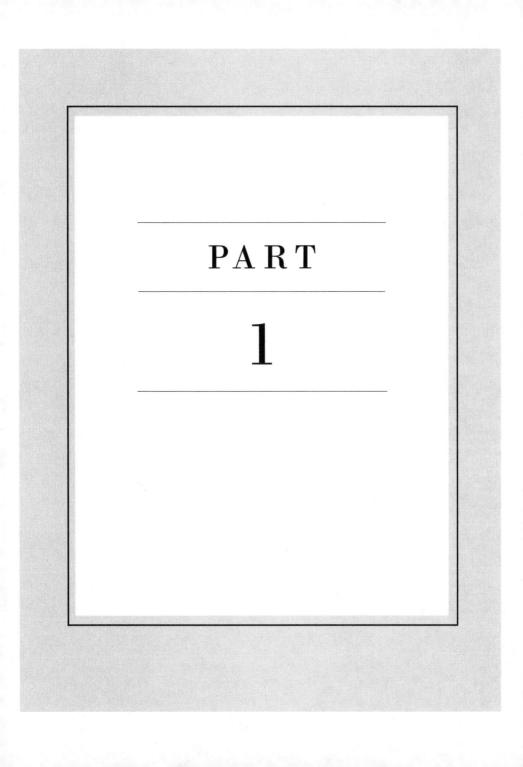

PART

1

BUILDING SAFETY

═══

"You belong"

YOU FEEL IT THE INSTANT YOU ENTER A STRONG CULTURE: that warm sense of cohesion, the shared willingness to speak up, the whole group thinking and feeling as one entity. We usually describe this phenomenon as "group chemistry," and tend to regard it as mysterious and accidental. But in fact, science has shown that group chemistry—or, to use the more accurate term, psychological safety—is not mysterious at all. Rather, it is built through the exchange of *belonging cues*—small, vivid behaviors that send a crystal-clear message:

- We are connected.
- We share a future.

- I care about you.
- You have a voice here.
- You matter.

Belonging cues signal our brains to switch out of vigilance mode, where we scan for possible danger, into connection mode, where we actively tune in to the people around us. That's why strong cultures send belonging cues in abundance, especially during critical moments when norms get established, such as the first time a group comes together, the group's first disagreement, and the first time the group learns something together. If you get these critical moments right—that is, if you flood the zone with belonging cues—you'll go a long way toward creating the foundation of safety on which strong culture is built.

One of my favorite belonging-builders is the Oscar-nominated director Ava DuVernay, who makes a practice of learning the names of her entire crew before the first day of filming. "I don't treat my actors differently than I treat the gaffer or the grip or the craft services manager or hair and makeup, because we're all making the movie," she told *The Statesman*. "No one is better than anyone else just because they're in front of the camera."

The actions that follow are a series of belonging generators. As you use them, keep in mind that your overarching goal is not merely to make people feel safe but to create an environment where everybody—from the newest hire to the CEO—knows they can speak up when it counts. "The academic research is overwhelming," says Amy Edmondson of Harvard, who pioneered the study of psychological safety. "When people believe they can speak up at work, the learning, innovation, and performance of their organizations is greater."

CONVERSATION STARTERS

Let's Talk About Safety

PSYCHOLOGICAL SAFETY IS POWERFUL because it's personal. You may experience a strong, warm sense of connection and belonging; the person next to you may be experiencing the opposite. As you explore these questions with your group, be sure to keep curiosity, perspective, and empathy foremost in mind.

On a scale of 1 to 10, how safe and connected do
people in our group feel? Does everyone in our group—
particularly members of historically marginalized
groups—feel the same way? If not, why?

_____

_____

_____

_____

Are we confident that people in our group know that
it's okay to speak up? How would we tell if they did
not feel that way?

_____

_____

_____

When someone new joins our group, how do we go about making them feel a part of it?

How do we build and sustain relationships with people who work remotely?

_____

_____

_____

"The beginning is the most important part of the work."
—Plato

TIP #1

Zero Tolerance for Brilliant Jerks

Brilliance is dazzling; that's why we tend to think that great performance can make up for bad behavior. But that belief is wrong: Studies show that the benefits of high-performing jerks almost never outweigh their cost to the group's performance.

Zero-tolerance policies work because they send a flashing-neon belonging cue: *Nobody, no matter how talented, is more important than the rest of the group.* And it works: Research shows that people in groups that value civility are 59 percent more likely to share information with one another than people in groups that don't. Here are three ways to jerk-proof your group, as well as to deal with occasional flare-ups:*

- **NAME IT:** Make it unmistakably clear in the hiring process that jerks are not welcome. One swift way to

---

* Some may ask: What about brilliant-jerk leaders like Steve Jobs, Elon Musk, Michael Jordan, and Thomas Edison? The answer is that brilliant jerks are indeed effective in rare cases, such as when they lead a group that holds a strategic advantage over the rest of the market. For the vast majority of groups, it works less well, because their people will simply leave for a competitor rather than endure jerk behavior. Even Steve Jobs stopped being a jerk when he realized how much it hurt the group.

do this is to add a jerk assessment. For example, the San Antonio Spurs evaluate hundreds of players each year for consideration in the NBA draft, assessing and measuring every factor—shooting percentage, speed, defensive skills, you name it. At the bottom of their evaluation sheet is a single line:

☐ Not a Spur

If this box is checked, they will not draft that player, no matter how talented they are.

To assess potential jerkhood, pay close attention to how the potential hire treats everyone—Zappos even debriefs the shuttle-bus driver who brings the candidate to the interview. Also, consider using these three questions, developed by Dylan Minor of the Kellogg School of Management at Northwestern University, which have been shown to indicate the likelihood that someone will engage in toxic behavior:

1. Which statement do you agree with more?
   A. The rules should always be followed.
   B. Sometimes you need to break the rules to get the job done.

2. You prefer most to:

   A. Ask others how they are doing.

   B. Move on from the past.

3. At work, do you see yourself more as:

   A. An innovator.

   B. A customer advocate.

(Answers B, A, and B indicate that someone is less likely to engage in toxic behavior.)

- **BROADCAST IT**: Send the "no jerks" message consistently and creatively. Paint it on your walls. Print it in the employee handbook—and name the specific behaviors that you will not tolerate (for example, condescension, rudeness, demands for special treatment). Repeat it in speeches, presentations, and town halls. The New Zealand All Blacks rugby team, one of the most successful sports teams of all time, has a mantra: "No Dickheads." Other groups use the "No Asshole Rule" to similar effect. It's simple and unmissable, and that's why it works.

- **CONFRONT IT**: If someone behaves like a jerk, call them out quickly and privately, spotlighting the behavior rather than the individual. If the pattern continues, don't hesitate to part ways. You can't eliminate all bad behavior. But you can send a consistent, unmistakable message that no one is bigger than the group.

TIP #2

Keep an Open Face

OPEN FACE

A VETERAN NAVY SEALS COMMANDER puts it this way: "Your face is like a door: It can be closed or open. You want to make sure you keep the door open."

He's talking about your expression—specifically the muscle above your eyes, which is called the frontalis. Using the frontalis—eyebrows raised, eyes alert and open—is how we signal attention, energy, enthusiasm, and engagement. Studies by psychologist Chris Frith show that signals from our eyes, brows, and forehead are perceived as more genuine and powerful than signals from our lower face, which are easily faked (think polite smiling). So when it comes to building safety, your frontalis is the most important muscle in your body—especially when you're working remotely and can't send as many physical cues.

TIP #3

Embrace Smart Icebreakers

Inside strong cultures, beginnings aren't merely beginnings: They are treated as vital moments when a sense of belonging is created, or not. That's why these cultures love to use that most underrated, clichéd tool of all: the icebreaker. You know, that supremely corny, cringe-inducing round-robin technique where individuals take turns answering personal questions in order to create cohesion. The keys to using them well are (1) to understand that the cringe is the point—the mutual vulnerability will draw you closer; and (2) to use them tactically, not indiscriminately. Here are a couple tips:

- Distinguish between icebreakers for Day One—the first time people meet—and icebreakers for project work, when people who already know one another are forming a team to work toward a specific goal. They may feel similar, but they have vastly different functions. Day One icebreakers are for getting to know colleagues as people—their likes, dislikes, interests—while the new-project icebreakers are for generating energy and clarity around the work itself.

For Day One:

Talk about what happens on your best days. How about your worst days?

When you think of your childhood, what meal comes to mind and why?

Tell me about your first car.*

For new projects:

What about this project excites you most?

---

*   Here are a few more:

- What are three things absolutely everyone should know about you?
- If we were stranded on a desert island, what skills would you bring to the group?
- If there were one song that was a soundtrack to your day-to-day life, what would it be?
- If you were to design a bar/restaurant, what and where would it be, and what would it be like?
- If you went on vacation tomorrow, where would you travel to first and why?
- Where are you from originally, and how many cities/places have you lived in for longer than twelve months?

What are you most wary of happening?

What skills are you most interested in building?

- Use the Pair and Share method: Rather than asking people to be vulnerable in front of the entire group, have people pair up to do their icebreaker privately, then have them share each other's answers with the larger group.
- Have the most powerful person in the room share first. This sets the tone and helps to normalize vulnerability (see Tip #24: Signal Fallibility Early and Often).

TIP #4

Actively Avoid Cool-Kid Bias

COOL-KID BIAS IS THE misperception that working in the physical office possesses more value, leverage, and impact than remote work. This bias is natural because it's rooted in our proximity-loving brains, and it's amplified by the assumption that being seen in the office is the best way to move up the ladder. While a certain measure of this bias is unavoidable, it can become toxic in large amounts, producing resentment, stoking fear, and creating an us-versus-them dynamic. Here are three antidotes:

- **Overcommunicate Office Happenings**
  Cool-Kid Bias is caused by informational asymmetry— so the remedy is to restore the informational balance.

Build a digital pipeline—a Slack channel or the like—that captures in-office happenings. Fill it with key events, breakthroughs, agendas, memos, questions, and even seemingly trivial developments (especially if they are funny or memorable). When in doubt if something should be shared, share it.

• Spotlight the Benefits of Working Remotely

Even as remote work has become normalized, it's easy to forget that it can create a sense of apartness and distance. Smart groups seek to lessen that distance by celebrating remote work's positive aspects. I was recently on a call when a leader made a point of celebrating several new babies who had arrived in remote workers' families, pointing out how good it was that these families could be together instead of coming into the office. It was a small moment but a powerful validation of the larger human value of working from home.

• Seek Gender Equity

Hybrid workplaces can magnify gender disparities because women tend to shoulder more household management responsibilities, creating a situation where men make up a higher percentage of in-person workers. This may lead women to feel that they don't belong and can also contribute to loneliness and stress. That's why it's vital for employers to provide scheduling flexibility for childcare and other obligations and to provide paid parental and family leave. In addition, consider having rotating office days, which helps ensure that everybody has access to in-person connections.

• Use In-Person Interactions Like a Booster Shot

It's no contest: In-person interactions are, by almost every measure, richer and more productive than their online versions, especially when it comes to creativity (see Tip #11: Divide Work into Two Buckets: Productivity and Creativity). Some all-remote groups, like the software-development operations company GitLab, offer subsidies for their remote workers to travel for multiday in-person visits with colleagues. These visits aren't focused on getting work done—they are about relationship building, which forms a foundation for connections and collaboration.

TIP #5

Obey the Two-Pizza Project Rule

WHEN IT COMES TO building project teams, it's tempting to believe that bigger is better—after all, having more brains makes a team smarter, right?

Wrong. Always aim to keep project teams to around six people. The reason resides in the math: A six-person team contains fifteen two-person relationships—a manageable number of interactions, where every member can contribute and share awareness. A team of twelve, on the other hand, contains sixty-six two-person relationships. Two-pizza teams hit the sweet spot: not too many relationships to manage but enough to generate creativity, connection, and belonging.

TIP #6

Make a Habit of Overthanking People

WHEN YOU GO INSIDE highly successful cultures, the number of thank-yous you hear seems slightly over the top. At the end of each basketball season, for instance, San Antonio Spurs coach Gregg Popovich takes each of his players aside and thanks them for allowing him to coach them. Those are his exact words: *Thank you for allowing me to coach you.* By all reasoning, this makes little sense—after all, both Popovich and the player are amply compensated, and it's not as if the player had a choice whether to be coached. But this kind of moment happens all the time in successful cultures because it's not just about expressing appreciation; it's also about affirming relationships and building belonging.

For example, when I visited KIPP Infinity, a highly successful charter school in Harlem, New York, I witnessed teachers thanking one another over and over. The math teachers received T-shirts marking Pi Day as a surprise present from the administrative assistant. Then Jeff Li, who teaches eighth-grade math, sent the following email to the other math teachers in the department:

> *Dear math teachers I love,*
>
> *On Assessment #7, a mid-unit test on linear functions (part of the foundational major work of the grade), the class of 2024 has outperformed the previous two classes on essentially the same test. See below for the data.*
>   *Class of 2018: 84.5*
>   *Class of 2023: 87.2*
>   *Class of 2024: 88.7*
>   *I know this is a result of better teaching at every grade level from 5th grade on . . . so thanks for being great teachers who are pushing to get better each year. It's working!*
>
> *—Jeff*

All this thanking has powerful downstream effects. In a study by Adam Grant and Francesca Gino, subjects were asked to help a fictitious student named "Eric" write a cover letter for a job application. After helping him, half of the participants received a thankful response from Eric; half received a neutral response. The subjects then received a request for help from "Steve," a different student. Those who had received thanks from Eric chose to help Steve more than twice as often as those who had received the neutral response. In other words, a thank-you caused people to behave far more generously to a completely different person. This is because thank-yous aren't only expressions of gratitude; they spark a contagious sense of safety, connection, and motivation.

"Good leadership requires you to surround yourself with people of diverse perspectives who can disagree with you without fear of retaliation."
—*Doris Kearns Goodwin*

TIP #7

Use the PALS Onboarding Method

ONE OF THE BIGGEST differences between weak and strong cultures can be seen on a new person's first day. Weak cultures approach onboarding as a check-the-box routine—*here's your parking pass and your healthcare forms*. Strong cultures, on the other hand, approach onboarding as an all-important opportunity to build safety and belonging. Here's a set of best practices I call the PALS method:

1. PERSONALIZED WELCOME: New arrivals are greeted warmly and see their name on a screen or a sign as they walk into the building—or, if working remotely, as they log on.

They are connected with an ambassador, who shows them the ropes and serves as a resource going forward.

2. ARTIFACT: New arrivals are given (or sent via mail, in the case of remote work) a token of appreciation: a meaningful book, a welcome note from leaders,* an item of clothing, or a symbol of the group's work. (At John Deere, new employees receive a miniature model of the first patented plow.) Something that says, *This is the start of something special.*

3. LUNCH WITH THE TEAM: New arrivals eat with a small group of colleagues—not to talk about work, but rather to create comfort and learn one another's stories. If you're remote, a virtual lunch date or an after-work happy hour will do. (It's even better if the company picks up the tab.)

4. SOLO MEETING WITH MANAGER: A quick check-in to build familiarity and reduce anxiety. A Microsoft study found that hires who had early meetings with managers built stronger networks, possessed a greater sense of belonging, and had higher long-term retention rates.

---

* On Day One at Apple, new hires receive a note that reads, in part: "People don't come here to play it safe. They come to swim in the deep end. They want their work to add up to something. Something big. Something that couldn't happen anywhere else. Welcome to Apple." On Day One at Pixar, new hires are brought into the auditorium, where the leaders say: "Whatever you did before, you are a moviemaker now. We need your help to make our movies better."

TIP #8

If Possible, Start in Person, Then Toggle

BLAME EVOLUTION ALL YOU like, but it's the truth: It's extremely difficult to build strong team relationships without any physical presence. Smart teams leverage this phenomenon by starting in person, then alternating short bursts of physical presence with longer stretches of remote work. The good news: It doesn't take much physical togetherness to build strong teams. At 37signals, the company that produces Basecamp software, remote teams meet up in person twice a year for four or five days each time. While they do some work during these in-person sessions—brainstorming, debriefing—their larger purpose is not to be productive but rather to generate shared understanding and to deepen relationships.

TIP #9

Embrace Deep Fun

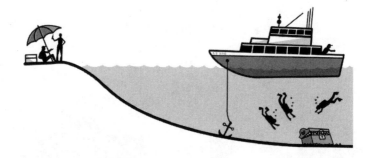

For years now, groups have sought to forge culture by filling offices with ping-pong tables, beanbag chairs, and happy hours. Despite this, engagement levels in these places barely budge. But there's a better way, and it's built on a simple distinction: Fun comes in two varieties, shallow and deep.

Shallow fun is the sugary, amusement-park enjoyment of doing pleasurable things together: games, laughter, and music. It affects groups like an adrenaline shot: It adds energy, then quickly wears off.

Deep fun, on the other hand, happens when people share ownership over the experience of group life. That is, they have power, make decisions, and hold responsibility. On the U.S. Women's National Soccer Team, players not only help choose and run practice drills but also design signature cleats for big games, as well as jerseys emblazoned with the names of their heroes (Malala, Serena, Ruth Bader Ginsburg). Not coincidentally, the team uses its collective power off the field as well, fighting in the courts to achieve pay equality.

Deep fun happens when you design your own workspaces, when you get involved in rethinking your group's onboarding process. It happens when your project team organizes its own off-site retreat, and when team members are given the freedom (and the funds) to give colleagues $25 gift certificates in appreciation for a job well done. And deep fun pays off: One study found that organizations that commit to deep-fun methods achieve more than four times the average profit and more than two times the average revenue of companies that focus merely on shallow engagement.

TIP #10

Make and Share "Best of Me" Documents

STRONG CULTURES POSSESS HIGH levels of collective self-awareness. That is, everyone in the group shares an understanding of the others' strengths, tendencies, and habits, which in turn helps drive group performance. One way to generate that awareness is to use a technique called a "Best of Me" document. In this, each person writes a one-page sheet that provides a snapshot of their values, preferences for communication, and activities that energize/exhaust them. Build it around four questions:

- I am at my best when _____
- I am at my worst when _____
- You can count on me to _____
- What I need from you is _____

"Part of being in a relationship means taking time to understand what each person needs," says Carmita Semaan, president of the Surge Institute, which develops and supports leaders of color in public education. "You've got to know what motivates and inspires them and what drives them crazy. The 'Best of Me' document is a blueprint that says, 'Hey, I can't change the fact that I'm a certain kind of person with certain strengths and weaknesses, but I can be honest about how I'm going to show up—about what you'll see from me, what I'll need, and what I'm encouraging you to call me on when you see it.'"

For project-based work, it's also useful to consider building a *team charter:* a co-created one-pager that maps out operating norms, roles and responsibilities, core values, methods of communication, and cadence of meetings—think of it as a "Best of Us" document. Whichever method you use, the aim is the same: to create clarity by bringing the unspoken stuff into the light early on so that you can all navigate better together.

TIP #11

Divide Work into Two Buckets:
Productivity and Creativity

IN ESSENCE, THERE ARE two types of work: (1) doing the regular stuff; (2) making new stuff. If you are seeking to be productive—that is, to do the regular stuff—working remotely has been shown to be more effective and efficient than working in person. However, if you are looking to innovate—that is, to invent new stuff—it's better to invest in physical togetherness. Studies show that a group of co-located workers talk about a problem eight times more often than remotely located workers, generating far more ideas. Divide your work into these categories and align your schedules accordingly. If your group needs to work remotely on a creative project, consider using Mural or another whiteboard app that allows the entire group to collaborate fluidly.

TIP #12

Share PDAs:
Public Displays of Appreciation

Cultures are strongest when they make relationships visible—and perhaps the fastest way to do this is through gratitude. Gratitude is powerful because, unlike most emotions, it energizes both the giver and the receiver. Specificity is key: Effective PDAs connect the dots between the action and the impact it had. "I appreciate Tonya's organizational abilities" works less well than "I appreciate Tonya's organizational abilities because it allowed our team to be more innovative, which led to [this specific breakthrough]."

Consider establishing a #Thanks channel so people can share appreciation publicly. Make sure it's highly visible and easy to share. A good #Thanks channel functions like a map, illustrating your group's warm relationships and spotlighting the sometimes-hidden connections that drive performance. And of course, stay conscious of your own bias to appreciate people who resemble you, and seek to express gratitude for the contributions of all people, in all roles. This especially applies to the emotional labor that can be easily overlooked, especially when it's performed by members of marginalized groups.

TIP #13

Embrace the Deep Work of Building Racial Equity and Belonging

Every group knows that diversity, equity, and inclusion matter. What separates strong cultures is that they aim for a higher goal: creating belonging. This distinction is best captured by using the metaphor of a party, as viewed by a member of a minority group.

> *Diversity and Equity* are when you get invited to the party.
>
> *Inclusion* is when you are asked to dance.
>
> *Belonging* is when you actively love the dancing.

Creating belonging across racial lines is no small project, and this playbook (written by a white male) won't come close to treating it comprehensively. However, we can explore how best to approach the challenge, and one place to start is to ask: What does belonging look like at its best?

Of the leaders I met, San Antonio Spurs coach Gregg Popovich, one of the most successful NBA coaches of all time, might be the most skilled at this. He approaches the challenge with an entrepreneurial mindset, continually seeking opportunities to talk about history, heritage, and the world beyond the basketball court. During one practice I witnessed, Popovich used the time normally devoted to analyzing game film to screen a documentary on the Voting Rights Act of 1965—and then facilitated an extraordinary whole-group conversation about it. At another practice just prior to the 2015 NBA Finals, Popovich created a conversation about Eddie Mabo Day—the Australian holiday celebrating a court case in which the indigenous people overturned a legal obstacle to land ownership.

"It made my hair stand on end [in a good way]," Patty Mills, a player who is indigenous Australian, told *Sports Illustrated* about the 2015 session. "It wasn't just any practice or meeting. It was to prepare for the NBA Finals and the Miami Heat. We're all geared up, and that's the first thing he says."

And that's the point. The connection was rooted in Popovich's endless curiosity to learn about cultures beyond his own and, more important, his willingness to spotlight their value. Here are a few ideas to consider as your group makes its own journey:

1. *Normalize Uncomfortable Conversations*

NOT SO LONG AGO, we lived in a world where difficult conversations about systemic racism, bias, and injustice simply didn't occur at work. The choice now is not whether to have these conversations but how to have them in ways that strengthen group culture. As conflict-resolution specialist Kwame Christian, the director of the American Negotiation Institute, puts it, "The best things in life are on the other side of a difficult conversation." To get there, it's useful to:

A. EMBRACE DISCOMFORT UP TOP

CONVERSATIONS ABOUT RACE AND equity are uncomfortable, especially at first, especially for members of the majority group. Normalizing that discomfort early in the conversation is one of the more important things you can do to normalize it. Saying,

We're all going to make some mistakes here because none of us are good at talking about this yet helps make the conversation safe.

A quick way to generate positive discomfort is the Althea Test, devised by consultant Anjuan Simmons.* It works like this: Ask the leaders of your group the following questions (if you answer "no" to any, you fail):

1. Do you know the names of the Black women who are individual contributors in your organization?
2. Can you list at least two contributions they made recently?
3. Do you see them doing your job eventually?

Also know this: *The discomfort is the point.* This work demands deep personal commitment to self-examination by each of us, and to noticing the set of feelings, dynamics, and reactions that we may have been blind to. It's not easy or fast, and acknowledging that difficulty both up top and throughout is critical. As Carmita Semaan of the Surge Institute says, "In living in discomfort, you grow."

B. ESTABLISH THAT THIS IS EVERYONE'S WORK

THERE'S A COMMON PHENOMENON in race-and-equity conversations where everyone assumes that the minority participants should do most of the sharing, while white people should

---

* The test takes its name from a woman Simmons worked with who was overlooked despite her contributions.

focus on listening and learning. That inevitably fails because it puts an unfair burden on members of minority groups (who now have to "explain" racism to their white colleagues). It's important that white people listen and learn with open minds, without defensiveness—but that alone will never solve the problem. At the same time, white people are often hesitant to speak out, fearful of making a misstep.

The solution? Bring the fears to the surface. We find an excellent example of this with the Penn State football team. After the George Floyd killing, they held a team meeting at which most of the talking was done by Black players. After the meeting, a white team manager named Michael Hazel shared his thoughts with the team in an email:

> *It is time for a few of us "white" guys to speak up in these settings; outside of Carl, none of us (white guys) spoke (player or staff member) . . . probably for a number of reasons. Fear is the main reason . . . fear of what some might think, fear of saying something controversial, fear of being misunderstood & even, maybe surprisingly, fear of retribution. If tolerance and progress are to be achieved, then we must give into vulnerability, walk into pressure and speak our minds. . . . We (white staff members) need to cultivate the courage to be uncomfortable and model to our younger (white players) how to accept discomfort as part of growth.*

Hazel's words—*accept discomfort as part of growth*—are powerful because they speak to the larger truth: This conversation asks everyone to dig deep and build resilience together.

C. EXPRESS GRATITUDE

Iт's not easy to have these conversations; good cultures—and especially leaders—seek ways to express thanks to those who have them, particularly those who shine a light on any problems or tensions within the group (see Tip #32: Hug the Messenger).

2. Read, Watch, and Reflect Together

The journey toward belonging and equity is about learning to see the world—especially yourself—through new eyes. That's why it's powerful to learn together: to watch a movie or read a book (I found *Waking Up White,* by Debby Irving, and *How to Be an Antiracist,* by Ibram X. Kendi, particularly effective), then have a conversation about it. Another way to do this is to take on Eddie Moore Jr.'s 21-Day Racial Equity Habit Building Challenge (https://www.eddiemoorejr.com /21daychallenge).

The challenge consists of twenty-one short readings, videos, and podcasts (each of which takes about thirty minutes), one per day. The syllabus covers the Black American experience through history, identity, and culture and serves as an engine for creating awareness, understanding, and conversation.

Be aware: This journey is long, deep, and personal. Kathleen Boyle Dalen, who co-leads racial equity diversity and inclusion initiatives at the Ewing Marion Kauffman Foundation, puts it this way: "If there was one thing I would tell people about this work, it's that this takes time. We started with ideas of time line, road map, deliverables—and instead we spend and still spend time doing the slow, uncomfortable work of building relationships, trust, talking about hard things. Letting people know to expect that up front will go a long way toward helping them figure it out."

3. Stop Saying "Culture Fit," and Start Saying "Culture Contribution"

SOMEWHERE ALONG THE LINE, the concept of "culture fit" became popular shorthand for assessing people, especially potential hires. The underlying idea is that people who slide effortlessly into a group's norms and styles add more value to the group than "poor fits." Thinking this way is a mistake because it amplifies your bias in favor of people who resemble you, and it puts you on a path to creating the most maladaptive, unsuccessful group of all: the monoculture. Which has an impact on the bottom line: According to a 2019 McKinsey study, businesses in the top quartile for racial and ethnic diversity are 36 percent more profitable than those in the bottom quartile.

So stop aiming for fit, and focus instead on contribution. Stop emphasizing what you share, and start emphasizing how you fit together to make the sum bigger than its parts. One way to start is by asking yourself and your team these questions:

- What new perspectives do we need to seek?
- Who can challenge us to get out of our comfort zone?
- What people or groups have historically been over-looked in our work?

4. Use "Who Am I" Speeches

THIS METHOD HAS BEEN used for years by the National Outdoor Leadership School to create connection among people who come from all walks of life. Each person gives a five-minute talk about themselves. Good speeches tend to include a few common elements:

- Key events that have defined who you are
- Something that people don't know about you and that would help people better understand you
- The moments, decisions, and events that have defined your extended family (after making sure everybody is comfortable sharing, of course)

The goal is to provide the group with a clear window into each other's whole person and then to keep that window open as you move forward.

5. *Gather Data, and Share It*

EQUITY IS ULTIMATELY NOT just an idea but a measurable outcome. Strong cultures track their progress using metrics of hiring and inclusion and also make a habit of gathering survey data that gives voice to the experiences different groups have.

Workday, a software company, does this through their Belonging Index, a survey that asks people to anonymously rate their responses to a handful of questions, such as:

- How happy are you at work?
- Do you feel like you have a voice here?
- How comfortable do you feel giving feedback to managers and others?
- How much are you learning and growing in your present role?
- How is your work-life fit?
- Do you receive meaningful recognition for doing good work?

Whatever method you choose, seek to support your conversations with measures of where things stand and which direction they are moving.

"Diversity drives innovation. When we limit who can contribute, we limit what problems we can solve."

—*Telle Whitney*

TIP #14

Use Flash Mentoring

MENTORING IS INCREDIBLY POWERFUL. It enriches a group's culture by forging relationships and by catalyzing deep learning for both the mentor and the mentee. The challenge is, traditional mentoring is a big ask, requiring large commitments of time and energy. The solution is to embrace flash mentoring, in which younger group members approach veterans with a low-stakes, can-we-grab-a-coffee request such as:

- I'm curious to learn more about how you prepared for that presentation.
- I'd love to learn what career advice you'd give your younger self.
- Can you take me behind the scenes of your last project? What went really well? What do you wish had gone better?

Small, well-targeted questions spark big conversations. For instance, whenever a new player was called up to the U.S. Women's National Soccer Team, former coach Jill Ellis gave them a task: *Go sit next to an older player and listen to their scars.* "There's so, so much for older players to teach younger ones," Ellis says. "Every successful player is successful because they've failed over and over again. Having younger players learn about that early on is so impactful."

During the conversation, mentees should keep in mind that the goal here is not to gain factual knowledge but rather to absorb how your mentor thinks—how they spot and conceptualize problems and opportunities. The goal is to get their voice inside your head so you can tap into it when you need to.

TIP #15

Take a Class Together

You might be surprised how many high-performing cultures spend time learning skills that have nothing to do with their work. I'm talking about skills like cooking, pottery, yoga, photography, you name it. Pixar goes the extra step with Pixar University, offering more than a dozen rotating classes on subjects like improv, sculpting, design, coding, and even juggling. All are held during the workday, with the shared understanding that it's fine to miss work to attend class. This works because the folks at Pixar know that learning and struggling together—newly hired assistants shoulder to shoulder with C-suite executives—flattens out hierarchies, creates serendipitous connections, and deepens relationships. Even better: Seek people in your group who are experts in a skill set and encourage them to teach it to the group.

TIP #16

Take a Regular All-Group Break

ONE OF THE SIMPLEST and most powerful things a group can do is to simply stop and take a break together. One design firm I studied has a tradition of ringing a gong to announce an all-group weekly coffee break. Others take a walk, or have an all-group lunch, or, as in the case of the Two Sisters Bakery in Homer, Alaska, close up shop so that the whole staff can attend the annual summer music festival (owner Carri Thurman even provides tickets and spending money). Synchronized breaks work because they generate the fabric of connection, conversation, and shared knowledge that knits groups together more tightly. One study at a Bank of America call center showed that shifting to synchronized breaks from randomized breaks tripled retention rates and improved performance by 23 percent.

TIP #17

Invest in the Best
Coffee Machine You Can Afford

(AND DON'T FORGET THE TEA.)

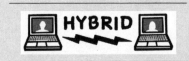

TIP #18

Make a Weekly Outer-Circle Phone Call

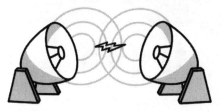

STUDIES SHOW THAT WORKERS who shift to remote tend to experience Shrinking-Circle Syndrome: They communicate more with people they already know well, and less with the more distant members of their network. This can lead to problems, especially since loose ties play critical roles in group creativity and career development.

The cure is to build the habit of having a once-a-week catch-up session with someone on the outer reaches of your circle. Send them a quick note suggesting the catch-up session, and consider using the phone. An old-fashioned audio connection can often create a deeper, more meaningful connection than video.

TIP #19

Use Heads-Up and Heads-Down Time

I T'S THE CHRONIC DILEMMA of physical work: open floor plan or private offices? Advocates for an open floor plan spotlight the importance of collisions, innovation, and flexibility; private-office proponents cite studies that show group interaction declines when open offices are introduced (presumably because everybody disappears under their headphones). What's more, research in this area is inconclusive, as it depends on the nature of the work being done. What to do?

The answer is to stop thinking about it as a space problem and start thinking about it as a time problem. Establish clear windows for group and solo work: heads-up and heads-down time. For instance, you can devote mornings to quiet work and afternoons to collaboration. Or use two-hour blocks. Or devote whole days to each—whatever works best, so long as you communicate it clearly. Also, consider permanently devoting certain areas of the office to heads-down work—the office version of Amtrak's Quiet Car—to provide for introverts who thrive with more privacy.

TIP #20

Pick Up Trash

Back in the mid-1960s, the UCLA men's basketball team was in the midst of one of the most successful eras in sports history, winning ten national titles in twelve years. After each game, John Wooden, the team's legendary head coach, would walk around the locker room after games, picking up trash. "Here was a man who had already won three national championships," said former student manager Franklin Adler, "a man who was already enshrined in the Hall of Fame as a player, a man who had created and was in the middle of a dynasty— bending down and picking up scraps from the locker room floor."

Wooden was not alone. Ray Kroc, the founder of McDonald's, was famous for doing the dirty work himself. "Every night you'd see him coming down the street, walking close to the gutter, picking up every McDonald's wrapper and cup along the way," former McDonald's CEO Fred Turner told author

Alan Deutschman. "He'd come into the store with both hands full of cups and wrappers. I saw Ray spend one Saturday morning with a toothbrush cleaning out holes in the mop wringer. No one else really paid attention to the damned mop wringer, because everyone knew it was just a mop bucket. But Kroc saw all the crud building up in the holes, and he wanted to clean them so the wringer would work better."

The leaders of the New Zealand All Blacks rugby team have formalized this habit into a team value called "sweeping the sheds." Their leaders do the menial work, cleaning and tidying the locker rooms—and along the way vividly model the team's ethic of togetherness and teamwork. Picking up trash is one example, but the same kinds of behaviors exist around allocating parking places (egalitarian, with no special spots reserved for leaders) and providing for equity in salaries, particularly for start-ups. These actions are powerful not just because they are moral or generous but also because they send a larger signal: *We are all in this together.*

TIP #21

Do a Reciprocity Ring

THIS BELONGING-GENERATING TECHNIQUE originated a few thousand years ago with New Guinea's Trobriand Islanders, but it still works like new. It consists of three steps:

1. Gather, in person or remotely, no more than twenty people.

2. One by one, each person shares a single small request with the group. The requests can be personal (Does anybody know a good dog-walker?) or professional (Can someone show me how to link documents in Slack?) or anything in between. The rule of thumb: Make requests that can be fulfilled in five minutes.

3. The rest of the group responds to the request, volunteering as they see fit. By the end, everyone has a chance to be both a giver and a receiver of help, and the room is brimming with gratitude and a fresh sense of connection. For more, check out Give and Take's knowledge-sharing platform Givitas at https://giveandtakeinc.com/givitas/.

> **"A leader's real authority is a power you voluntarily give him, and you grant him this authority not with resentment or resignation but happily."**
>
> —*David Foster Wallace*

TIP #22

Set Aside Time to Do Nothing Together

GOSSIP IS CULTURAL GLUE. While you'll want to avoid its morale-sapping mean-spirited form, you want to nurture the continual organic flow of informal chatter, the BS sessions, the sharing of intelligence that boosts group connection and awareness levels. That's why high-performing remote teams set aside time for *just hanging out*—eating, chatting, doing stuff that has nothing to do with their jobs and that helps them get in sync with one another. At Google, remote teams break for tea together at the same time every day. The restaurants Per Se and French Laundry are located thousands of miles from each other in New York and Napa Valley, but their kitchens are connected via live camera so each can see the other in real time. Other groups use coffee roulette, a weekly gathering that randomly places people into hangout groups of four to six people.

Two keys to remote hangouts: (1) be ready to talk about things that have nothing to do with work; (2) be ready to feel supremely awkward the first time you eat together on camera. But once you get used to it, you'll see how fun and natural it can be—because breaking bread together, physically or virtually, remains one of the most connective experiences a group can have.

> # BUILDING YOUR GAME PLAN:
> ## STEP TWO

STRENGTHENING OUR SAFETY

A SENSE OF SAFETY IS rooted in simple, repeated behaviors that send an unmistakable signal: *I see you. You have a voice here. You belong. We share a future.*

Individual Activity #1

MAPPING SAFETY

IN GROUPS, SAFETY WORKS like oxygen: It's the invisible energy source that makes everything possible.

1) List the initials of the people you work closely with.

_____

_____

_____

_____

_____

_____

_____

_____

_____

_____

YOUR TURN

2) Place their initials on the map according to your sense of safety in that relationship.

Individual Activity #2

QUESTIONS FOR REFLECTION

Name one behavior you could do tomorrow to increase
the sense of safety and belonging in your group.

_____

_____

_____

_____

Think about one person in your group who does not
speak up as often as they might. What could you do
to let them know their voice is needed and appreciated?

_____

_____

_____

YOUR TURN

_____

_____

_____

_____

At your group's next remote meeting, what question
might you ask to create a stronger sense of connection?

_____

_____

_____

_____

_____

YOUR TURN

Group Activity

THIS THIRTY-FIVE-MINUTE SESSION IS designed for groups of four to eight people. Larger groups should divide up accordingly, then share their results with one another.

> **MATERIALS:** Sticky notes, a marker, and a whiteboard (or the digital equivalents)

1. Have each person select two actions they would like to try from the list below. Write the title of each on a sticky note and post it on a whiteboard. (five minutes)

THE ACTIONS

Zero Tolerance for Brilliant Jerks

Keep an Open Face

Embrace Smart Icebreakers

Actively Avoid Cool-Kid Bias

Obey the Two-Pizza Project Rule

Make a Habit of Overthanking People

Use the PALS Onboarding Method

If Possible, Start in Person, Then Toggle

Embrace Deep Fun

Make and Share "Best of Me" Documents

Divide Work into Two Buckets: Productivity
  and Creativity
Share PDAs: Public Displays of Appreciation
Embrace the Deep Work of Building Racial Equity
  and Belonging
Use Flash Mentoring
Take a Class Together
Take a Regular All-Group Break
Invest in the Best Coffee Machine You Can Afford
Make a Weekly Outer-Circle Phone Call
Use Heads-Up and Heads-Down Time
Pick Up Trash
Do a Reciprocity Ring
Set Aside Time to Do Nothing Together

Or create your own:

1. _____

2. _____

3. _____

2. Ask each person to explain what drew them to these actions and what impact they may have. (ten minutes)

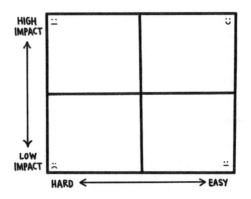

3. As a group, use your collective wisdom to locate each action on the matrix above. The goal is to identify two to three actions that are in the upper-right quadrant: highly impactful and easy to do. (ten minutes)

4. Now that you've chosen your two to three actions, name the specific steps you should take in order to implement these actions. What will you do tomorrow? What tools or materials do you need? Who should you include in the conversation? (ten minutes)

Action #1 _____

Steps

_____

_____

_____

_____

_____

Action #2 _____

Steps

_____

_____

_____

_____

Action #3 _____

Steps

_____

_____

_____

_____

YOUR TURN

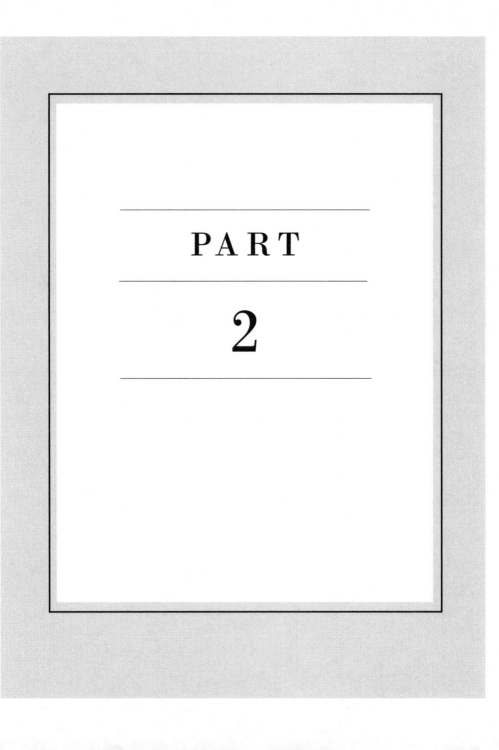

PART

2

SHARING
VULNERABILITY

"We trust"

WHEN YOU WATCH A STRONG CULTURE IN ACTION, YOU witness many moments of trusting cooperation. Without communication or planning, the group starts to move and think as one, finding its way through problems in the same way that a school of fish finds its way through a coral reef, as if they are all wired into the same brain. It's beautiful.

If you look closely, however, you will see something else. Sprinkled amid the smoothness are moments that don't feel so smooth or beautiful. These moments are clunky, difficult, and full of hard conversations. They contain pulses of profound tension as people deal with obstacles and struggle together to figure out what to do.

These moments are called *vulnerability loops,* and they are the heart of the trust-building process. Vulnerability loops happen when two or more people come together to admit they don't know the answers, to share weakness. They are based on a powerful psychological truth: When people take interpersonal risks together, they connect and cooperate far more deeply.

Normally, we think about trust and vulnerability the same way we think about standing on solid ground and leaping into the unknown: First we build trust, then we leap. But strong cultures show us that we've got it backward. Vulnerability doesn't come after trust—it comes before. Taking a risk, when done together, causes the solid ground of trust to materialize beneath our feet.

Making the first move requires boldness. One of my favorite examples is from Melinda Gates, co-chair of the Gates Foundation. A few years back, seeking to rejuvenate group trust, Gates made an in-house video in the style of "Celebrities Read Mean Tweets" in which she read her own performance reviews—choosing the most critical ones to read first. The first review included the line "Melinda is like Mary Effing Poppins—so perfect in every way." After laughing, Gates then opened up, good-naturedly listing her own flaws and shortcomings, modeling the sort of humility that creates connection.

Expect to feel discomfort as you take these actions—after all, that's the point. Also expect that you'll get accustomed to this feeling as you go on—you may even come to welcome it. Building trust in your group works exactly like building muscle in your body: No pain, no gain, and the more you do it, the stronger you get.

CONVERSATION STARTERS

Let's Talk About Vulnerability

WE ARE TAUGHT THAT we need to trust before we can be vulnerable, but in fact we have it backward: Moments of vulnerability, when shared, create trust, cohesion, and group chemistry.

Name one elephant in the room that your group
needs to have a conversation about.

_____

_____

Describe the typical response in your group when
someone makes a big mistake or fails. Why does that
happen?

_____

_____

_____

_____

_____

Think about the closest, most trusting relationships
you have within your group. What actions and habits
make them strong?

Think about all the ways your group comes together,
both virtually and in person. Which of those gather-
ings tends to strengthen relationships? Which tends
to weaken them?

Makes Us Stronger	Makes Us Weaker

Makes Us Stronger	Makes Us Weaker

TIP #23

Kill the Happy Smoothness Fallacy

PERHAPS THE MOST COMMON misconception about successful cultures is that they are tension-free sunshine-filled places where disagreements are rare and mistakes are few. This is not remotely true. In fact, successful cultures don't transcend tensions; they embrace them and use them as cultural fuel. They continually lean into uncomfortable conversations, navigate disagreements, and embrace their mistakes—because they understand that their strength springs from how they navigate problems together. In other words, happy smoothness isn't a feature; it's a bug to be overcome. Here are a few ways to do that:

1. *Call Out Smoothness as a Negative.* If you hold a meeting with zero questions or disagreements, you should point out that it's been unproductive—after all, if everybody agrees, why did you get together to talk? If all the

feedback is positive, why did you seek it? Conflict and
tension are not problems to be avoided; they are opportunities for your group to figure things out together.

2. *Distinguish Between Relational Conflict and Task
Conflict.* All conflict is not created equal. Relational
conflict—me versus you—is personality oriented,
emotional, and almost always unproductive. Task
conflict—my ideas versus your ideas—is an engine
for innovation and should be cultivated. When you
encounter tension, always seek to ask: *How can we
make this about the ideas and not about the people?*

3. *Make It Safe to Talk About Mistakes.* When we make
mistakes, our overwhelming instinct is to conceal, ig-
nore, and move on. Strong cultures flip that dynamic.
They seek to highlight and remember their mistakes
and use them as navigational markers, focusing on the
clarity the mistakes created and the new paths they
sent people on.

One of the best leaders at doing this is voting-
rights advocate Stacey Abrams, who follows three
rules: (1) give people stretch assignments; (2) let
them know she expects some mistakes; (3) create
space to learn from those mistakes.

"I knew that if I didn't have an answer to something, I wasn't going to be hung out to dry," Aiko
Bethea, who worked with Abrams on Atlanta's Gov-
ernment Counsel team, told *Business Insider.* "So I
never had a worry about getting it wrong and being
punished for it or shamed for it. . . . It's about giving

your team members permission to learn and to grow. Underneath that means that yeah, you're going to fail. That's just part of the expectation, because I want you to learn. I want you to grow. I'm going to give you the opportunities to do so."

4. *Define and Leverage Your Group's Core Tensions.* Every group continually encounters a handful of core tensions. Perhaps it's a tension between innovation and tradition (Should we lean into the new or stick to well-established ways of doing things?), between serving the customer and supporting staff (When should we put the client first, and when should we tend to our teammates?), or between focusing on succeeding now and investing in the future (Should we support existing projects or focus on R&D?).

These tensions aren't a negative—they are actually the crux of your work, the steep parts of the mountain you're climbing together. Defining and spotlighting them sends a clarifying, energizing signal: *Yes, these tensions are really hard, and navigating them together—and embracing these difficult conversations— is what helps us be successful. After all, if this stuff were easy, everybody would do it.*

TIP #24

Signal Fallibility Early and Often

WHEN I VISITED PIXAR, I toured a relatively new studio building with Ed Catmull, the company's co-founder and president.
It was a stunningly beautiful building, brimming with mind-
bendingly creative art and sunlit gathering spaces. As we
walked, I said, "Ed, this is the coolest building I've ever seen."

Catmull stopped, turned, and looked me square in the eye.

"Actually," he said, "this building was a mistake."

I was shocked. "Really?"

"Yes," Catmull said evenly. "It doesn't create the kinds of
interactions we need to create. We should have made the hall-
ways wider. We should have made the café bigger, to draw more
people. We should have put the offices around the edges to create more shared space in the center. So it wasn't like there was

one mistake. There were really a lot of mistakes, along with of course the bigger mistake that we didn't see most of the mistakes until it was too late."

I remained stunned. When you compliment most leaders on their beautiful buildings, the majority of them say, "Thanks." But not Catmull. Why?

A few weeks later, I found the answer. I was in Virginia Beach, Virginia, having breakfast with Navy SEAL Team 6 command master chief Dave Cooper. Cooper is known for creating some of the most cohesive SEAL teams, including the ones that killed Osama bin Laden. Midway through breakfast, Cooper said this:

"The most important words a leader can say are, *I screwed that up.*"

Bingo. Like all good leaders, Catmull and Cooper know that signaling fallibility is the all-important start of a vulnerability loop, that powerful moment when a group shares its weaknesses in order to get stronger. They know that weak cultures hide their problems; strong cultures reveal them so that they can be solved together. Here are a few ways to do that:

1. *Explicitly Ask for Help.* It's not enough merely to admit you don't have all the answers. You also have to actively invite people to jump in and help. Here are some phrases that are useful:

   • I'd love for everybody to take some shots at this idea.
   • Tell me what we're missing here.

- We're definitely going to get some things wrong here.
- This is just our first try—what will take this to the next level?
- I need you to poke some holes in this.

Precisely what phrase you use doesn't matter—so long as it contains a clear signal: *I need your help to make this better.*

2. *Frame Fallibility Around Learning.* One common hesitation about expressing fallibility is that it risks signaling incompetence. The solution is to frame your fallibility around a desire to improve. So use phrases like *I'm really curious to learn more* and *Who in our group can tell us more about this issue?* and *Can you teach me how to do that?*

3. *Seek to Have Strong Opinions, Flexibly Held.* You might think that people in strong cultures have strong opinions—and you're right. But here's the thing: They combine that passion with a deep openness to the possibility that they might be wrong. They take strong positions but never fight to the death. I like the phrase "backbone of humility" because it captures the paradoxical nature of this quality: combining the enthusiastic strength to make your case with a profound, continual willingness to learn from others. As Mary Barra, CEO of General Motors, likes to say, "It's okay to admit what you

don't know. It's okay to ask for help. And it's more than okay to listen to the people you lead—in fact, it's essential."

> **"Example is not the main thing influencing others; it is the only thing."**
> —*Albert Schweitzer*

TIP #25

Hold a Premeeting Warm-Up

Aᴛ ᴛʜᴇɪʀ ᴡᴏʀsᴛ, ᴏɴʟɪɴᴇ meetings are dull, awkward spaces in which a few people talk while everyone else switches off their cameras and tunes out. This creates an environment where truths can get buried and where voices are muffled or silenced, particularly those voices belonging to people from marginalized groups. That's why it's essential to use warm-ups: short activities that create a warm, shared mental space. "Virtual is voluntary," says Glenn Fajardo, who studies remote work at Stanford's Design School and is co-author of *Rituals for Virtual Meetings*. "If you want them to engage, you need to get them actively creating something or, better, creating in groups. You have to tap into intrinsic motivation; create a pull dynamic."

Fajardo recommends warming up by using five-minute break-out rooms with no more than four people each. Give everybody a prompt: *What was the best meal you ate this week? What's one thing you're looking forward to this month? What's the best movie you ever saw?* "Keep the prompt light and positive, and don't make it about work," Fajardo says. "The goal is to let people take it where they want to take it."

Some alternative warm-ups:

- **THE FIFTEEN-SECOND LIGHTNING ROUND:** A small-group method in which everybody shares a two-sentence personal update. Consider using a two-part format: one life update and one thing they're excited about at work.
- **THE ENERGY CHECK:** First, ask everyone in the group to rate their present levels of energy and focus between 1 (barely awake) and 7 (superalert). Then, ask them to make one change in their environment that will boost their score by one point. They might stand and stretch, switch off phone notifications, grab a cup of tea—it doesn't matter, so long as everyone is tuning in to the act of being together.
- **BREATHING:** Take a few deep breaths together.
- **MUSIC:** Share a playlist or, better, have everyone submit a song beforehand. Then play the songs while the group guesses who submitted each one.
- **SMELLS:** Ask everybody to smell the same spice at the same time and share their reactions (sounds weird, I know, but it works).

Caveat: Don't feel compelled to use warm-ups for every meeting (which can be a drain on those who are in all-day back-to-back remote meetings). Rather, target them for situations where you are aiming to be creative together or are reconnecting with people you haven't seen in a while.

TIP #26

Send the Three-Line Email

THIS IS ONE OF my favorites because it's so simple. It originated with Laszlo Bock, CEO and co-founder of Humu, and it goes like this: Send an email to your team containing these three questions:

- What is one thing I currently do that you'd like me to continue to do?
- What is one thing that I don't currently do frequently enough that you think I should do more often?
- What can I do to make you more effective?

They are short questions, but they send a big trust-strengthening signal—*Please help me improve*.

You may find that this signal is contagious. When one person asks for useful feedback—especially if it's a leader—others will do it too. And, to make the connection even stronger, schedule in-person meetings to go over the replies, rather than using email.*

> ## "The art and science of asking questions is the source of all knowledge."
>
> —*Thomas Berger*

---

* Here are four more trust-building questions, courtesy of leadership consultant Jean Marie DiGiovanna:

What's the thing you see me doing that's helping me best contribute to the team?

What's one thing I need to know about you that will improve our relationship?

What's one gift, skill, or talent you have that I've overlooked, undervalued, or underutilized?

What motivates you, and how can we bring more of that to your work?

TIP #27

When Listening, Use the Magic Phrase

LISTENING TO EACH OTHER'S problems—really listening—might be the most powerful culture-building skill on the planet. It's also difficult to do, because when someone brings us a problem, we all feel the same overwhelming instinct: to help, now. We try to add value, to share a story about a similar situation, to provide resources. We stop listening, and we start talking. We can't help it.

There's a better way, and it starts with the most magical trust-building phrase ever invented: *Tell me more*. These three words work because problems are like icebergs: small and simple on the surface, massive and complex beneath. Before you can help, you need to probe and to learn: What led to this problem? What else like this is happening? Where do you think this is headed? Who else could help? *Tell me more.*

Your goal is to "surface the tension," a concept used by Roshi Givechi, a former team facilitator at IDEO: to transform a one-way response into a two-way dialogue in which people explore questions, connect useful dots, and create understanding together.

Jack Zenger and Joseph Folkman, who run a leadership consultancy, analyzed 3,492 participants in a manager development program and found that the most effective listeners do this:

1. They interact in ways that make the other person feel safe and supported.
2. They take a helping, cooperative stance.
3. They occasionally ask questions that gently and constructively challenge old assumptions.
4. They make occasional suggestions to open up alternative paths.

In other words, the most effective listeners behave like trampolines. They absorb what the other person brings, support them, and add energy to help the conversation gain velocity and altitude. When asking questions, they rarely stop at the first response. Rather, they keep adding energy, seeking to explore an area of tension, in order to reveal the truths and connections that will help uncover the path forward.

TIP #28

Build the AAR Habit

I‌F YOU USE JUST one tip from this book, this is the one. The After-Action Review is a trust-building tool rooted in a simple truth: Talking together about the strengths and weaknesses of your performance makes your group better. Originating in the military, the AAR was perfected by the Navy SEALs, for whom it forms the foundation of their extraordinary teamwork.

It works like this: Just after your group finishes an important task—maybe a project, a sales call, even a meeting—you circle up and create a conversation around three questions:

- What went well?
- What didn't go well?
- What are we going to do differently next time?

The goal is not to assign credit and blame but rather to create clarity so the group can learn together. "It's got to be safe to talk," SEAL Team 6 leader Dave Cooper says. "Rank switched off, humility switched on. You're looking for that moment where people can say, 'I screwed that up.' You have to resist the temptation to wrap it all up in a bow, and try to dig for the truth of what happened, so people can really learn from it." And that learning adds up: Francesca Gino and Bradley Staats performed an experiment where one training group spent fifteen minutes a day reflecting on their work; a second group spent an extra fifteen minutes working. After fifteen days, the reflective group performed 20 percent better on a skills test.

Some groups also use a Before-Action Review, which is built around a similar set of questions:

- What are our intended results?
- What challenges can we anticipate?
- What have we or others learned from similar situations?
- What will make us successful this time?

One more tip: It may be useful to follow the SEALs' habit of running the AAR without leadership involvement, to boost openness. Likewise, it may be useful to write down the findings—particularly what will be done differently next time—and share them across the group. After all, the goal of an AAR is not just to figure out what happened but also to build a shared mental model that helps the group navigate future problems.

"Change is a behavioral epidemic,
not an information tsunami."
—Leandro Herrero

TIP #29

Take Virtual Hallway Walks

IN THE PHYSICAL WORLD, the postmeeting hallway walk is one of the most connective moments in any group: It's where people catch up, share what they're thinking, and process problems together. With remote work, it takes intention. Make plans to do a virtual hallway walk with one or two colleagues, ideally just after a meeting has ended. Don't have an agenda; simply reflect together.

One of my favorite conversation structures is the What? / So What? / Now What? model. First, focus on mutually understanding the event (What did you notice? What stood out?). Then, talk about its meaning (What's the impact? How does this change our situation?). Finally, examine possible courses of action (What might happen next? What should we be focusing on going forward?).

TIP #30

Ask the Magic Wand Question

OF ALL THE TRUST-BUILDING actions, one of the most effective is also the simplest. Ask each member of your group: *If you could wave a magic wand and change one thing about the way we work, what would it be?*

The answers might be about vacation policy, the offboarding process, the office layout, snack offerings, or anything under the sun. For leaders, the key is not just to listen to the answer but to help make the suggested change happen as swiftly as possible.

My favorite example of this method is from Michael Abrashoff, a navy captain who took command of the destroyer USS *Benfold* in 1997. At the time, the *Benfold* ranked at the bottom of the navy's performance scores. One of Abrashoff's first acts was to hold a thirty-minute one-on-one with each of the ship's 310 sailors. (Completing all the meetings took about six weeks.) Abrashoff asked each sailor three questions:

- What do you like most about the *Benfold*?
- What do you like least?
- What would you change if you were captain?

Whenever Abrashoff received a suggestion he felt was immediately implementable, he announced the change over the ship's intercom, giving credit to the idea's originator. On the strength of this and other culture-building measures (which are detailed in Abrashoff's book *It's Your Ship*), the *Benfold*'s performance levels improved to the point where it became one of the navy's highest-ranked ships in three years—providing us with a concise lesson on how to empower a group: *Ask what needs changing, then change it.*

TIP #31

Avoid Brutal Honesty,
Embrace Warm Candor

THIS WILL BE A **TOUGH EXPERIENCE** — BUT WE'RE IN THIS **TOGETHER.**

WE'VE ALL HEARD IT, that leathery phrase people use when they deliver tough feedback: *Look, I'm going to be brutally honest with you.* This approach feels authentic, but it has a huge downside—it creates a culture of brutality.

Better to aim for warm candor, when you deliver two signals at once: connection *and* truth. I saw a good example of warm candor one afternoon at Gramercy Tavern, a top-ranked New York restaurant. On the day I observed, Whitney Macdonald was minutes away from a moment she had long anticipated: her first-ever shift as a front waiter. The lunch crowd was lining up on the sidewalk, and she was excited and a bit nervous. Assistant general manager Scott Reinhardt approached her—for a pep talk, I presumed.

"Okay," Reinhardt said, fixing Whitney with a bright, penetrating gaze. "The one thing we know about today is that it's not going to go perfectly. I mean, it *could,* but odds are really, really, really high that it won't."

A flicker of surprise traveled across Whitney's face. She had trained for six months for this day, learning every painstaking detail of the job, hoping to perform well. She had worked as a back server, taken notes, sat in on lineup meetings, and shadowed shift after shift. Now she was being told in no uncertain terms that she was destined to screw up.

"So here's how we'll know if you had a good day," Reinhardt continued. "If you ask for help ten times, then we'll know it was good. If you try to do it all alone . . ." His voice trailed off, the implication clear—*It will be a catastrophe.*

Reinhardt was delivering a hard truth—today will be tough, and you will make mistakes. And he was also sending a vivid signal of connection: *You are not alone. Expect to make mistakes and to learn from them. We're all together in this.*

TIP #32

Hug the Messenger

ONE OF THE MOST powerful moments in group life happens in the instant after someone shares bad news or gives tough-to-hear feedback. In these moments, it's important not simply to tolerate the difficult news but to embrace it.

"You know the phrase 'Don't shoot the messenger'?" says Harvard professor Amy Edmondson. "In fact, it's not enough to not shoot them. You have to hug the messenger and let them know how much you need that feedback. That way you can be sure that they feel safe enough to tell you the truth next time."

Of course, hugging the messenger—and to be clear, hugging in this case is purely metaphorical—is just the first step. Equally important is how you talk about that moment with the rest of the group. Don't conceal the difficult news; spotlight it. Tell everyone how much you appreciated getting it and how much you need to keep getting it to improve in the future.

TIP #33

Build a Failure Wall

WEAK CULTURES HIDE AND minimize their mistakes and pretend they never happened. Strong cultures leverage their mistakes to create learning. One way to do that is to build a failure wall: a prominently placed space on which you capture and commemorate your group's missteps.

Methods vary: Some groups cover a wall with Post-it summaries of their mistakes or scrawl them on a whiteboard wall. Others devote a date to celebrate failed projects (some tech companies deem this their "Day of the Dead"). Others award a rotating trophy to the biggest fail of the week; still others share Failure Résumés, in which each person lists all their professional goof-ups. Whatever method you choose, seek to ensure that your leaders share their failures early and often, and leave room for new ones to be added. The goal is not to wallow in the mistakes or to assign blame but rather to nurture the group habit of reflecting on where you went wrong, learning from it, and, most of all, continually broadcasting the signal that it's not merely safe to experiment—it's essential.

TIP #34

Hold a No-Secrets Meeting

I T'S THE KIND OF meeting every group dreams of: a gathering of total transparency where all the status, hierarchy, and ass-covering vanishes, and the group provides one another—and especially its leaders—with an unvarnished look into what's really happening on the ground. The good news is that it's possible: I've seen groups of surgeons, teachers, athletes, and special-ops soldiers benefit profoundly from the learning and increased awareness that such no-secrets meetings create. The trick is that these meetings are also tough to pull off because they can easily slide into the culture-destroying zone of grievance, recrimination, and personal attacks. So here are a few ground rules:

1. *Define the purpose clearly up top.* Make it crystal clear that the goal is not to vent but rather to share concrete knowledge that helps everyone do their job better. Set firm guardrails—no personal attacks—and encourage everybody to come prepared to share (1) areas where they are struggling and (2) insights that might help others improve.

2. *Get away.* Go offsite, or to any location where people don't have to worry about being overheard or observed. And keep it small: Big groups aren't as effective as groups that are under ten people.

3. *Focus on generating awareness.* At their best, no-secrets meetings are about creating fresh perspective—and about making room for the positive as well as the negative. Here are three questions that might help:

- What do you think I need to know that I don't?
- Where are you struggling?
- What are you proud of?

Be sure to share gratitude, both during and after the meeting. You may find that the biggest awareness your group creates is a fresh appreciation for the power of the relationships within it.

TIP #35

Give Tours of Personal Workspaces

ONE FAST WAY TO amplify warmth, especially in newly formed groups, is to encourage people to pick up their laptops and show others around their workspace. This "widens the window," allowing the group to see one another as whole people, not just as faces on a grid. Even better: Pick a favorite photo or a personal object and share the story behind it. And of course, be aware of and sensitive to the fact that some people may be in situations that make sharing difficult or impossible.

TIP #36

Normalize Mental Health Conversations

IF ONE OF YOUR co-workers broke their leg, your group would reach out to support them. Mental health issues should receive the same response, but they are harder to detect, especially in remote work. Strong cultures seek ways to bring mental health conversations into the open and check in on one another in a caring, nonjudgmental way. Here are three ways to do that:

- **Model Openness**

When it comes to normalizing mental health conversations, few forces are more powerful than the actions of a leader. Senior leaders at Genentech, a biotech company, created a series of short videos talking about their own mental health, then followed up by training "mental health champions" to create conversations about the subject. I met one leader of a hedge fund who went one step further by sharing the story of his own mental challenges with his group. "I was scared to do it," he said. "But it turned out to be the best thing I ever did as a leader."

- **Do Remote-Work Check-Ins**

In the physical world, it's relatively easy to detect whether people are having a good or bad day/week/month. In the remote world, however, you need to take the extra step and ask.

In a small group (six or fewer), ask if everybody is comfortable doing a well-being check-in. Ask people to rate their stress levels and energy levels from 1 to 5 and then share their answers with one another—it's best if leaders go first. Create a no-pressure space for people to share the reasons they are feeling this way, if they so choose. (For another approach, please see Tip #43: Hold an Anxiety Party.)

It's important to focus on the positive aspects of mental health as well as the negative. Golden State Warriors coach Steve Kerr likes to use the invented metric of Zest For Life, rated from 0 to 100. "How's your ZFL?" Kerr will ask, and the other person will share their numbers—perhaps today it's 91; yesterday it was 76. It creates an easygoing exchange that takes only a few seconds and can lead to deeper conversations.

- **Share Resources**

Place links in prominent places; frame them in a positive way and, if appropriate, share success stories that the resources enabled. Seeking mental health advice should not feel like something to be ashamed about; it should feel like visiting a coach.*

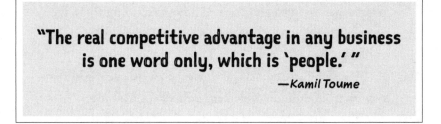

"The real competitive advantage in any business is one word only, which is 'people.' "
—Kamil Toume

---

* Two useful resources in this area are activeminds.org and mhfaengland.org.

TIP #37

Hold an Idea Exchange

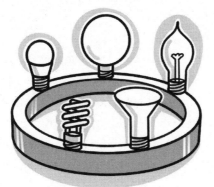

ONE OF THE MOST transformative moments in any group's life is when it suddenly sees itself from a new perspective. The swiftest way to achieve this is through an idea exchange: a single day when two like-minded organizations come together to compare notes, explore common challenges, and learn from each other. Here's how to do it.

- *Reach out to an organization that shares a key aspect of your skill set.* For example, I've seen idea exchanges between Green Beret officers and General Electric leaders on effective communication, and between professional sports teams and trauma surgeons on how to perform under pressure. Pick someone in an adjacent lane, a noncompetitor who's facing some of the same challenges. Be sure to keep the group relatively small—under ten people or so—to give everyone a voice and to keep the conversations manageable.

• *Be open about your group's challenges and shortcomings.* This is not a time to display your strengths but rather a time to be honest with yourself about where you fall short. What are you struggling with? What tools are you seeking to improve?

• *Use the 2+2 Framework.* Ask each participating group to preselect two topics they want to explore for one hour each, then add another two hours for emergent conversation and relationship building. The topics work best if they bridge a gap between your group's weakness and the other group's strengths. *Your group is incredible at locating and hiring talent—and we struggle to do that. Can you walk us through your approach and process?* Whatever format you choose, the goal is always the same: to walk away with new ways of seeing and thinking, and to cultivate a wider, deeper network of relationships.

Perform Regular Team Tune-Ups

Iᶠ ʏᴏᴜ'ʀᴇ ᴀʀᴏᴜɴᴅ ʜɪɢʜ-ᴘᴇʀꜰᴏʀᴍɪɴɢ teams, you'll notice that they possess a dual focus. Half of their attention is firmly on the project at hand, while the other keeps a sharp eye on the team's inner workings. Like race-car drivers, they make regular pit stops to tune the group's engine and fill its fuel tanks.

One way to achieve this, pioneered by the design firm IDEO, is called the Flight Check-In system. It involves team meetings held before, during, and after the project. Like After-Action Reviews (see Tip #28), they seek to help the team see the work clearly. Unlike AARs, they place an explicit spotlight on the team's inner workings, creating conversations that surface and improve team dynamics. Here's a template:

PREFLIGHT: WHAT WE AIM TO DO

- Define the objective, roles, and responsibilities.
- Discuss communication flow and decision-making.
- Talk about areas where each person wants to grow and learn.
- Do a pre-mortem: If we are looking back a year from now and wondering how this project failed, what happened?

MIDFLIGHT: HOW'S IT GOING?

- Ask everyone to share one word to describe the team's performance so far.
- Ask everyone to share one thing the team should do more of.
- Ask everyone to share one thing the team should do differently.
- Inquire if the project's scope has shifted—and if so, how.

POSTFLIGHT: WHAT WE LEARNED TOGETHER

- Co-create a document describing what you learned in this project—especially any tools or processes that could be scaled.
- Ask everyone to share one shout-out (something a teammate did well).

The deeper benefit is located not just in increasing your team's self-awareness but also in building the organizational habit of carving out time to create a conversation about the most vital, continual questions you face: *How well are we working together? How might we get better at it?*

TIP #39

Play the Subtraction Game

ONE OF THE CHRONIC challenges every culture faces is the Disease of More. It's rooted in the fact that modern life invariably adds more tasks than it subtracts; the result is that we are steadily buried under an ever-accumulating avalanche of New Stuff We Have to Do Now. Stanford professors Bob Sutton and Hayagreeva Rao have developed a cure called the Subtraction Game, which works like this: Periodically hold a fifteen-minute meeting with your team where you ask the following questions:

- What are we doing that was once useful but is now in the way?

- What is adding needless friction?
- What is scattering your attention?

Sutton and Rao have found the game works well if you ask people to answer the questions in three stages: first individually, then in small groups, then sharing out to the large group. Also, be sure to include leaders who have the leverage to enact the changes immediately. The payoff is not just improved efficiency but also a shared realization: *We have the power to change things around here.*

TIP #40

Ask the More/Differently Questions

FEEDBACK IS ONE OF the key pillars of high-performing cultures—and it's also one of the trickiest. How does the giver ensure that their feedback is useful and accurate? How does the receiver avoid feeling judged or marginalized? And we all know that the oft-used "feedback sandwich"—the technique of layering one negative between two positives—is way past stale.

One of the best feedback tools I've encountered is a framework used by Ellen Van Oosten, who teaches leadership at Case Western Reserve University and is the co-author of *Helping People Change*. Her idea is to flip the conversation away from giving feedback and focus instead on creating reflection through two questions:

- What do you think you should do more of?
- What do you think you might do differently?

In other words, instead of pushing feedback on someone, seek to create a reflective pull. These questions work because they do what good coaching does: They spotlight the positive, avoid judgment, generate autonomy, and orient growth.

TIP #41

Deliver Negative Stuff in Person

THIS IS A BELOW-THE-RADAR rule that I encountered at several high-performing cultures, and it goes like this: If you have negative news or feedback to give someone—even as small as a rejected item on an expense report—you are obligated to deliver it face-to-face—or, with remote work, in a one-on-one video call. This rule is not easy to follow—after all, it's easier, faster, and more comfortable to type the message. But it works because it handles tension in an up-front, honest way that creates shared clarity and connection.

One of the most creative methods for handling negative stuff is that employed by Joe Maddon, longtime major-league baseball manager and avowed wine connoisseur. In his office, Maddon keeps a glass bowl filled with slips of paper, each inscribed with the name of an expensive wine. When a player violates a team rule, Maddon asks them to draw a slip of paper out of the bowl, purchase that wine, and share it with their manager. In other words, Maddon links the act of discipline to the act of reconnection. He understands that moments of negativity are where cultures can fall apart—and they're also where they can become stronger.

TIP #42

Take a Curiosity Time-Out

THIS ONE WORKS AS a midmeeting energizer for remote work, and it goes like this.

1. Partway through the meeting, announce the time-out: "Given the purpose of this meeting is _____, what is one thing that you're curious about?"
2. Give everyone twenty seconds to reflect quietly.
3. Ask everyone to share their answers verbally with the group, keeping them short and clear—a couple sentences, maximum.

The goal is not to merely answer their questions but to use the questions to light up new paths of awareness and exploration. Plus, it helps your group realize that seemingly awkward moments of silence aren't really awkward—they're the sound of your group thinking together.

TIP #43

Hold an Anxiety Party

THIS STRESS-REDUCING, trust-generating technique was invented by teams at Google Ventures, and it's especially effective with remote work. It works like this:

1. Gather in a small group, either remote or in person, no more than six people.
2. Each person spends ten minutes writing down the small handful of work-related issues they worry most about, then stacking them from most to least concerning.
3. Each person shares their list with the group, which then scores each worry from 0 (a nonissue from their point of view) to 5 (deserving of concern and attention).

4. For any worry that averages higher than a 3, the group spends time brainstorming possible strategies and solutions together.

You'll find that the party serves as a pressure-relief valve, as well as a platform for people to connect and solve problems together. It also goes a long way toward normalizing conversations about stress, anxiety, and mental health (see Tip #36: Normalize Mental Health Conversations).

TIP #44

Share Your Backhand

STRONG CULTURES SEEK WAYS to spotlight the skills and abilities they want to improve. One way to do this is called "sharing your backhand." The idea comes from racquet sports, where we all have certain skills that are stronger (our forehands), and those that are weaker (our backhands). At Next Jump, an e-commerce company, new employees attend a leadership boot camp at which they identify their forehands and backhands and then share them with the group. "Sharing backhands can become really normal," says Meghan Messenger, co-CEO of Next Jump. "When you expose a weakness and talk about it, it's amazing what happens. People start talking, going to each other for help. It moves you away from the illusion of perfection and makes the messiness of being a human being into the norm— and that connects everybody." Are you skilled at brainstorming creative projects but do you struggle with the disciplined execution? Do you thrive in solo work but struggle with cooperation? Sharing your backhand creates shared awareness, outlines potential developmental pathways, and generates safety because, after all, everybody has one.

TIP #45

Fill the Bleachers

ONE OF THE MORE underrated features of remote work is the ease with which people can be added to a meeting—creating a zero-cost opportunity for observational learning. Consider designating a few "bleacher seats" at big meetings for emerging leaders, interns, and others who might be interested in watching and learning. The goal is not to have the people in the bleachers participate, merely to have them observe how leaders in your group communicate, think, and interact. Then be sure to follow up afterward to see what the bleacher-dwellers noticed—your group might learn something new.

TIP #46

Mark the Ends of Projects

WHEN WE COMPLETE A group project, we often feel a strong instinct to mark it DONE and click over to the next item on our to-do list. This is a mistake. Strong cultures carve out time to take a breath together and mark the transition, to appreciate the things that went well, and to learn from the things that didn't (see Tip #28: Build the AAR Habit).

It doesn't need to be fancy. The actor/director Amy Poehler has a tradition of ending every project with a daisy-chain series of toasts: Each person makes a toast to one other person in the group, who then toasts someone else, and so on. I've seen other groups write each other notes of appreciation, and of course there's the path of celebratory dinners and the like. Whatever you choose, so long as it's authentic, connective, and fun.

TIP #47

Practice Healthy Offboarding

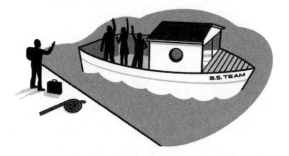

THE TWO MOST CRITICAL moments in any culture are when someone joins and when someone leaves. That's why strong cultures treat offboarding with the same degree of intention and care that they bring to onboarding (see Tip #7: Use the PALS Onboarding Method). Here are three principles to follow:

- *Maximize the Warmth.* Departures are no fun. We feel a powerful instinct to pull back, to minimize. Strong cultures, however, do the opposite. They create platforms for people to share appreciation and good memories and to wish the person well. This message, of course, isn't just for the departing person: It's also a signal of connection and safety for the rest of the group. The navy uses a tradition called Hail and Farewell: a dinner at which the outgoing person is honored with toasts, gifts, and remembrances. The particulars vary widely: Some are black-tie formal, others family picnics. The central message remains the same: *We see you, we appreciate you, we are grateful for the time we shared.*

• *Be a Springboard.* The most powerful moments happen when the group actively supports the departing person with tools to help them be successful. The legendary San Francisco 49ers coach Bill Walsh made a habit of giving departing coaches videos and playbooks along with the message: "Here is your tool kit for your new job." Most coaches would have viewed the playbook as proprietary information to be protected. But Walsh knew that his team's success couldn't be distilled to mere information and that there was far more to be gained by supporting the person in their new endeavor. He also knew that people often return, and it never hurts to help someone feel good about the way they leave.

• *Get the Download.* The moment someone decides to leave, they see the organization from a new perspective. Strong cultures capture that perspective in a frank and thorough exit interview: What are we missing? What could we do better? What issues and challenges are people not willing to talk about that we should be talking about? Departing people are one of your group's richest learning resources—so don't let them walk away untapped.

TIP #48

Have Leaders Occasionally Disappear

Here's a surprising sight you see at successful cultures: At certain moments, the leader quietly disappears, leaving the group to figure things out on its own. One of the best at this is San Antonio Spurs coach Gregg Popovich. Most NBA teams run time-outs according to a protocol: First the coaches huddle as a group for a few seconds to settle on a message, then they walk over to the bench and deliver that message to the players. However, during about one time-out a month, the Spurs coaches huddle for a time-out . . . and then never walk over to the players. The players sit on the bench, waiting for Popovich to show up. Then, as they belatedly realize he isn't coming, they take charge, start talking among themselves, and figure out a plan.

The New Zealand All Blacks rugby team has made a habit of this, as players regularly lead practice sessions with little input from the coaches. When I asked Navy SEAL Team 6 command master chief Dave Cooper to name the single trait that his best-performing SEAL teams shared, he said, "The best teams tended to be the ones I wasn't that involved with, especially when it came to training. They would disappear and not rely on me at all. They were better at figuring out what they needed to do themselves than I could ever be."

BUILDING YOUR GAME PLAN:

STEP THREE

STRENGTHENING OUR VULNERABILITY

GETTING BETTER AT GROUP vulnerability is like building a muscle. Discomfort is not a downside but rather an essential part of the growth.

Individual Activity #1

CONVERSATION BUILDER

VULNERABILITY DOESN'T COME AFTER trust—it precedes it. Taking a risk, when done alongside others, causes the solid ground of trust to materialize beneath our feet.

(A dashed oval with two horizontal lines inside for writing.)

1. In the center of the circle, name one conversation your group should be having but isn't. Focus not on airing grievances but on ways that you might improve together.

2. Around the outside, write the names of the people who would play a helpful role in that conversation.

Individual Activity #2

QUESTIONS FOR REFLECTION

With regard to the conversation you named in Activity #1: What are some ways that you might open the door to that conversation?

_____

_____

_____

_____

_____

Think of a story about a time you screwed up and learned something that helped you in the long run. Now name some people in your group—perhaps new members—who might benefit from hearing that story right now.

_____

_____

_____

_____

YOUR TURN

YOUR TURN

Think about the best listener you ever met. If you could "borrow" one skill from them and make it your own, what would it be? How would you put it to use?

_____

_____

_____

_____

_____

Group Activity

THIS THIRTY-FIVE-MINUTE ACTIVITY IS designed for groups of four to eight people. Larger groups should divide up accordingly, then share their results with one another.

MATERIALS: Sticky notes, a marker, and a whiteboard (or the digital equivalents)

1. Have each person select two actions they would like to try from the list. Write the title of each selection on a sticky note and post it on a whiteboard. (five minutes)

THE ACTIONS

Kill the Happy Smoothness Fallacy

Signal Fallibility Early and Often

Hold a Premeeting Warm-Up

Send the Three-Line Email

When Listening, Use the Magic Phrase

Build the AAR Habit

Take Virtual Hallway Walks

Ask the Magic Wand Question

Avoid Brutal Honesty, Embrace Warm Candor

Hug the Messenger

Build a Failure Wall

Hold a No-Secrets Meeting

Give Tours of Personal Workspaces

Normalize Mental Health Conversations

Hold an Idea Exchange

Perform Regular Team Tune-Ups

Play the Subtraction Game

Ask the More/Differently Questions

Deliver Negative Stuff in Person

Take a Curiosity Time-Out

Hold an Anxiety Party

Share Your Backhand

Fill the Bleachers

Mark the Ends of Projects

Practice Healthy Offboarding

Have Leaders Occasionally Disappear

YOUR TURN

Or create your own:

1. _____

2. _____

3. _____

2. Ask each person to explain what drew them to these actions and what impact they may have. (ten minutes)

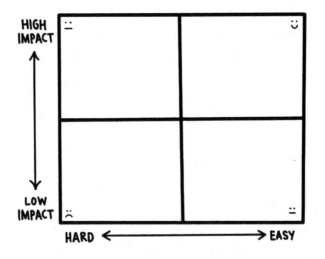

3. As a group, use your collective wisdom to locate each action on the matrix above. The goal is to identify two to three actions that are in the upper-right quadrant: highly impactful and easy to do. (ten minutes)

4. Now that you've chosen your two to three actions, name the specific steps you should take in order to implement these actions. What will you do tomorrow? What tools or materials do you need? Who should you include in the conversation? (ten minutes)

Action #1 _____

Steps

_____

_____

_____

Action #2 _____

Steps

_____

_____

_____

YOUR TURN

YOUR TURN

Action #3 _____

Steps

_____

_____

_____

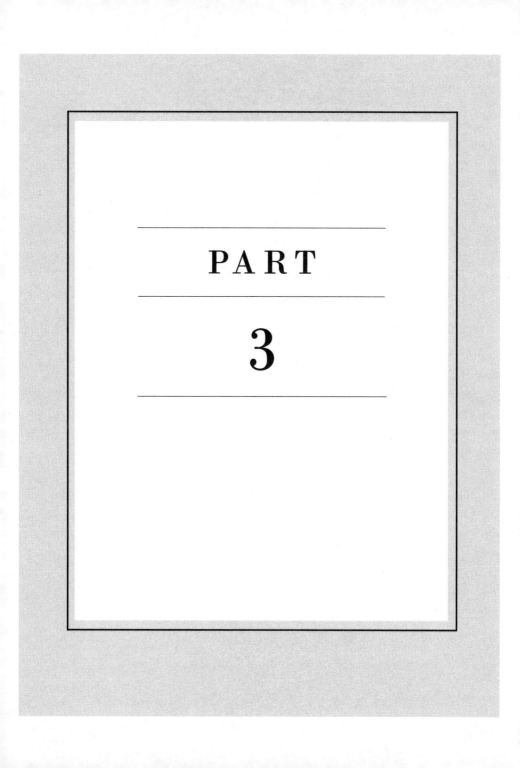

PART

3

ESTABLISHING
PURPOSE

———

"Finding true north"

BUILDSING A SUCCESSFUL CULTURE is like embarking on a wilderness expedition. You need teamwork. You need stamina. Above all else, though, you need clarity. You need a reliable way to help your group navigate through the disorienting, distracting thickets of daily life and find true north. That's where purpose comes in.

When most people think of purpose, they think of solemnly worded statements issued from on high. In fact, creating a sense of purpose is more extensive, more collaborative, and more organic. It's not about carving a single mission statement into granite; it's more like building a set of bright spotlights that illuminate your path forward. The spotlights consist of a rich, ever-evolving set of images, catchphrases, behaviors, stories, and artifacts that help your people know where they are, where they are going, and why it matters. Accordingly, the actions that follow take many forms, but they all involve the same process: to continually reflect together about what matters most, and then to translate that meaning into signals that are visible, tangible, and felt.

As you go about creating your group's sense of purpose, there's one more thing to keep in mind: the overarching importance of building your purpose on a foundation of optimism and hope. Strong cultures are about moving toward a positive vision, never about running away from a negative one. "Optimism is a core principle of good leadership," Disney CEO Bob Iger once told an interviewer. "People don't want to follow someone who is a pessimist."

CONVERSATION STARTERS

Let's Talk About Purpose

PURPOSE ISN'T LOCATED IN any single phrase—it's in the whole kaleidoscope of stories, mantras, symbols, sayings, behaviors, and images that fill your group's windshield, continually guiding you toward your highest goals.

Imagine that someone flew in from Mars to observe your group. How would they know what mattered most to you? How would they detect your highest priorities?

_____

_____

_____

If you asked the people in your group to describe
the group's biggest, most important goal, would
their answers be similar or different? Why?

_____

_____

_____

_____

_____

_____

What is the single story that captures the essence
of your group at its best?

What would happen in your group if your leaders
did not show up for one week? What would be the
best-case scenario? The worst-case?

Embrace Corny Catchphrases

YOU MIGHT ASSUME THAT strong cultures would not use corny catchphrases. You might assume that they would be unshakable and clear-eyed about their purpose and would not require cheesy sloganeering.

In fact, it's precisely the opposite. From the SEALs ("The Only Easy Day Was Yesterday"; "The Quiet Professionals"), to Zappos ("Create Fun and a Little Weirdness"; "Embrace and Drive Change"), to KIPP schools ("Whatever It Takes"; "All In for Every Student"), strong cultures use corny catchphrases with generous abundance, painting them on the walls, writing them in handbooks, repeating them in speeches, and filling the air with them so much that visitors can find it overwhelming.

The reason is that catchphrases aren't merely catchphrases; they are signals that orient attention and energy and connect the present moment to a larger sense of shared meaning and direction. They signal: *This is why we work. Here is where you should put your energy.* Unlike mission statements, which are generic and hard to recall, effective catchphrases have a few basic qualities:

- They're short and vivid.
- They spotlight a key action or attribute.
- They're easily remembered and shared.

When you're creating catchphrases, the goal is not to be clever but rather to be clear and natural. Start by seeking out existing catchphrases and amplifying them. And if you're looking for ways to generate them, see the next tip.

TIP #50

Create a Mantra Map

IN 1985, DANNY MEYER opened his first restaurant, and it was a success. A few years later, he opened his second, and within a few months both restaurants had started to falter. Why? Because Danny Meyer *was* the culture, and he couldn't be in two places at one time. When Meyer was in the room, the team could sense what mattered, what didn't, and how to behave. When Meyer wasn't in the room, the culture started to evaporate. After Meyer heard that one of his waiters had insulted a customer, he knew he had to act. He needed to lift his cultural values into the light and make them utterly explicit.

He started building a set of simple phrases that captured the benefits he wanted to create, as well as the behaviors he wanted to nurture. Here is what it looked like:

CREATING RAVES

Read the guest
Athletic hospitality
Writing a great final chapter
Turning up the home dial
Loving problems
Finding the yes
Collecting the dots; connecting the dots
One size fits one
Making the charitable assumption
Put us out of business with your generosity
Be aware of your emotional wake
To get a hug, you have to give a hug
The excellence reflex
Are you an agent or a gatekeeper?

Note the top line: Meyer starts by defining true north as *Creating Raves*—two vivid, powerful words that go far beyond merely "serving great food" or "being successful." Then he goes on to define the key behaviors—*finding the yes, loving problems, athletic hospitality*—the actions that propel the group toward its goal. The result is the equivalent of a socio-emotional map: *Here is the goal, and here is how to get there.* He began teaching the map, and using it to assess potential hires, to train staff, and to define and spotlight the precise set of skills and reflexes he needed his team to possess.

What Meyer did can be done by any group. Here's how:

1. Gather up. If you're a large group, break into tables of six to eight people. Share Meyer's story and mantra map with the whole group.

2. Ask each table to generate your culture's version of Meyer's map. What is your group's true north? What phrases capture the key behaviors to help you get there? What problems do you face over and over, and how do people ideally respond to those problems? What behaviors should *never* happen? Encourage people to generate as many mantras as possible, the cornier the better.

3. Ask each table to share their maps with the larger group, capturing the results on a whiteboard or an easel. Share the results, asking questions and creating conversation. What are we missing? Is this who we really are? Communicate frequently with your team about what the mantras mean and explore different ways to weave them into your work. Mantra maps aren't meant to be forever; they're an awareness tool, and they change over time. To this day, Meyer is still writing mantras to address new challenges and opportunities. You'll find that the same is true for your group.

TIP #51

Do a Best/Barrier Workshop

THIS IS ONE OF my favorite exercises because it generates clarity and energy through two simple questions: *What do we look like at our best? What is stopping us from doing that every day?* (And yep, you might recognize this one from the "Building Your Game Plan" questions on page 13.) It takes about an hour.

1. Divide the group into tables of six to eight people (maximum five tables), and ask each table to spend ten minutes discussing question 1: *What do we look like at our best?* Describe specific instances in which your group performed at its highest level—the behaviors, the communication, the patterns of interaction.

2. Ask each table to share their responses with the rest of the room, capturing the result on a whiteboard or an easel (twenty minutes).

3. Now ask each table to spend ten minutes exploring question 2: *What keeps us from doing that every time?* Name the barriers that prevent your culture from performing at its highest level—the more specific the better.

4. Ask each table to share their answers with the larger group (twenty minutes). The goal is not to be judgmental but rather to start an ongoing conversation about the challenges and opportunities of the landscape you all share.

TIP #52

Start Each Meeting by Linking to Your Group's Purpose

MEETINGS ARE WHERE PURPOSE goes to die. That's why it's wise to set aside a brief moment at the start of each meeting to swiftly spotlight the larger purpose of the work—the "big why." It doesn't take much—a couple quick sentences connecting the dots between the events of today and your group's larger purpose. At Ochsner Health, a chain of hospitals, they do this by telling a patient story at the start of every meeting. Some are stories of success; others illustrate challenges. All highlight the relationship between Ochsner's staff and the lives of its patients, and thus orient the meeting around what really matters.

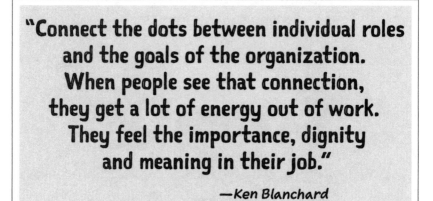

"Connect the dots between individual roles
and the goals of the organization.
When people see that connection,
they get a lot of energy out of work.
They feel the importance, dignity
and meaning in their job."

—Ken Blanchard

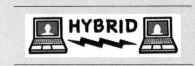

TIP #53

Build the Habit of a Postmeeting Reflection

Remote work can feel like swimming in an endless ocean of identical-feeling conversations. That's why it's vital to carve out a few minutes after each meeting to stop, rewind, and consider what just happened. Think like a detective. Who was particularly quiet, or effusive? What topics sparked the most energy from the group? Where might the conversation go next? Jot down your observations and review them occasionally. The goal is not to arrive at definitive answers but to use the questions like a flashlight, so you can see more deeply.

TIP #54

Share a Weekly Impact Note

ONE OF THE MOST powerful beacons any culture can use is a vivid spotlight on what greatness looks like. One way to spotlight greatness is through a Weekly Impact Note. This consists of two steps:

1. Capture specific instances of your group's positive impact on clients, customers, and community—the benefits it brings to the world.

2. Share those stories with your group on a regular basis. I encountered a Maryland medical office that solicits patient feedback after visits. They handle the negative feedback (about one in ten responses) through service-recovery channels. The positive feedback is shared back to the group,

topped by an appreciative paragraph from the clinic leader. The notes are simple and specific—*Thank you for the kindness and friendliness . . . I appreciated Ashley's professional, top-notch care . . . Dr. Dunleavy was extremely competent and attentive*—and that's why they work, orienting the group toward the most effective behaviors.

These kinds of anecdote-based tools tend to be undervalued because they lack the satisfying thump of metrics. But that's precisely the point. Their intangible quality is what generates meaning, emotion, and identity. We think and feel in story, not numbers. Speaking of which . . .

TIP #55

Treat Stories as a Precious Resource

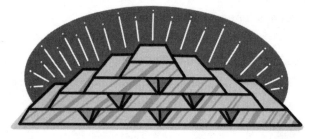

STORIES ARE THE MOST powerful force on the planet. They light up our brains—assigning value, igniting emotion, providing models for behavior—and stick in our memories twenty-two times more powerfully than mere information, according to Jennifer Aaker of Stanford Business School. That's why strong cultures seek to cultivate and sustain a rich web of stories that capture and illustrate their values, skills, and strengths, and even their weaknesses.

For example, I've met several leaders who like to tell a particular type of story that might be titled *Tales of My Youthful Missteps*. One successful general manager of a major-league baseball team often tells it to new hires, and it goes something like this:

"When I started here, I headed up a project that analyzed catching fundamentals. I worked for months, gathering piles of all this amazing data and putting it all together. I thought I had everything figured out—that is, until I went down to the dugout and spent fif-

teen minutes talking to our major-league catcher. That was when I realized: I was missing so much! There was a ton of nuance about catching—a million little decisions and details—that I didn't understand, that I needed to learn from the people who actually do the job on the field." The general manager gives a big smile. *"I was way, way off! I didn't have a clue!"*

The story, and the smile, deliver a clear message: *Data is powerful only if you understand where and how it's applied.* They also send a warm signal: *I made mistakes, and you will too, and that's okay.*

Think of your group's stories as its collective cultural memory—sort of like a shared photo album you turn to when you want to boost connection and clarity. Here are a few ideas on how to do that.

- *Target the Story to Your Group's Need:* Different stories are suited for different situations. In addition to Youthful Misstep stories, here are a few types to use.

   If your group is struggling with motivation, consider using **Impact Stories,** which connect the dots between your work and the benefit it creates in the world. For example, I once saw a bolt manufacturer tell a story about how their product held a helicopter propeller to the fuselage during a crash, saving the life of the pilot. Even more powerfully, the group took the extra step of inviting the pilot to a conference and bringing her onstage. The audience was brought to tears because they got a clear signal: *Our product saves lives.*

   If your group needs to reconnect with its roots, you

may want to consider **Crisis Stories,** which capture the defining moments in which your group's culture was forged. Leaders at Pixar frequently tell the story of the near-death and resurrection experience that ensued when the company decided to abandon a complete but medio-cre straight-to-video version of *Toy Story* and to reshoot the entire movie in record time for a full theatrical release. The story serves as a vivid reminder of what it means to set a high bar (as the Pixar mantra says, "B-level work is bad for the soul") and helps guard against complacency.

If your group is disconnected or losing touch with its values, consider **Virtue Stories,** which capture instances when people take risks and make sacrifices to do what is right. For example, I've heard many groups tell moving stories about how members cared for one another and family after an unexpected illness.

If your group is struggling to solve hard problems, you may want to consider **Innovation Stories,** which showcase out-of-the-box thinking and open new channels of exploration. One Navy SEAL commander I know likes to tell a story about how his team, unable to travel incon-spicuously through crowded Pakistani streets, hit on the idea of hiding inside a local jinga truck—a wildly painted, bead-covered local bus that resembles something you might see at Burning Man—to reach their target. It's an unforgettable story—especially when you picture a team of geared-up SEALs crammed into a psychedelic van— and it highlights an energizing notion: *The best idea might be under our nose.*

- *Hold CSWD meetings:* This stands for Cool Stuff We Do, a regular meeting where the goal is to share stories of energizing events happening across the organization. Scheduling an hour a month for telling and listening to stories about you at your best might be one of the best investments your group can make.

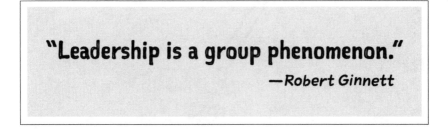

"**Leadership is a group phenomenon.**"
—*Robert Ginnett*

TIP #56

Do a Culture Capture

STRONG CULTURES DO CULTURE captures for the same reason you get a yearly physical exam. It's a big-picture check-in that gives you a sense of where you stand and helps you spot any incipient problems. Here's how to do it:

1. Survey everyone in your group with the following questions (use a survey-collecting tool, such as SurveyMonkey, which allows you to keep responses anonymous):

    • Besides succeeding, what do we want to accomplish as an organization?

- What is your top reason for working here?
- Describe our culture in three words.
- What about us is so central and fundamental to our culture that we should never change it?
- How are we different from the competition? What separates us?
- What are the non-negotiables in our culture? What will we not stand for?
- Briefly share a story about something that happened in this organization that would not happen anywhere else.
- Name one thing you would change about our culture.
- What big issue hasn't been covered in this survey, one that is important to understanding our culture and where we're headed?

2. Create a spreadsheet that lists your group's core values across the top. Now collect the survey answers and bucket them into the core value to which they apply most, either supporting it or challenging it.

3. Share the resulting document back to the group, with a summary memo of its findings. Ask: Where are we strong? Where are we weak? What tensions need to be embraced? What should we consider changing?

   The goal is to create an ongoing conversation about how well the group is living up to its values. As you do so, don't be afraid to challenge your existing culture to change. In fact, many of the leaders I met did this instinctively, cultivating what might be called a productive dissatisfaction. They were mildly suspicious of success and unafraid to ask hard questions like *Do we still believe this? Is this who we really are?* In asking those questions, and making it safe for others to ask them, you avoid complacency and create room for growth.

Use Artifacts

WHEN YOU WALK INTO a strong culture, you instantly sense its purpose. For example, when you walk into SEAL headquarters at Dam Neck, Virginia, you pass a twisted girder from the World Trade Center and so many memorials to fallen SEALs that it resembles a military museum. Similarly, walking into Pixar's headquarters feels like walking into one of its movies: From the full-size Woody and Buzz made of Legos to the twenty-foot-tall Luxo Lamp outside the entrance, everything gleams with Pixarian magic. At the San Antonio Spurs, home of the "Pound the Rock" mantra, the first thing you see on entering is—you guessed it—a large boulder and a hammer.

Your group doesn't need an illustrious history to achieve this. Simply seek to represent the benefit you create in the world: It could be displaying oversize emails from happy customers, or naming a conference room after your group's inspiration, or capturing a piece of your history and displaying it in a glass case. The point is to fill the physical space with vivid reminders of your purpose—to spotlight what matters so that everyone can feel it.

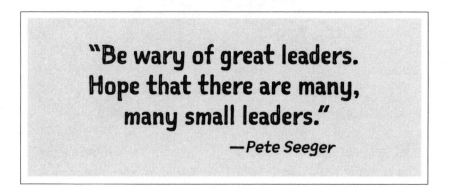

"Be wary of great leaders.
Hope that there are many,
many small leaders."
—Pete Seeger

TIP #58

Play the Nine Whys Game

Pᴇʀʜᴀᴘs ɴᴏ ғᴏʀᴄᴇ ᴇʀᴏᴅᴇs a group's sense of purpose more than the never-ending busy-ness of modern life; that rushing river of small, urgent tasks that wash away our time and attention. How do you know what's important when *everything* feels important?

That's why I like the Nine Whys Game created by Henri Lipmanowicz and Keith McCandless. It provides a group a chance to stop and create a clearer sense of what matters and what doesn't. It takes about an hour, and it goes like this:

1. Pick one big task or project that your group works on together.
2. Ask the group to list all the activities they do to accomplish that task or project.
3. Go through the activities one by one. Ask: What impact does this have? Why is that important to us?

Why does it matter? Keep digging deeper—it may take up to five or six or even nine whys—until you agree that you have reached the fundamental purpose of each activity, and thus the work.

4. Look ahead. Ask: How does our purpose influence the next steps that we take together?

You may find that some of your activities in fact don't contribute to the purpose; you may find that some contribute massively. The goal is to emerge with a clearer sense of where to put your energy.

TIP #59

Create a Culture Book and/or Deck

Fundamentally, establishing purpose is about making meaning—and there's no better way to make meaning than to build a shareable representation of your group's purpose that can be used both to orient new group members and to reorient everyone else to the meaning of your work. The good news is that there are lots of useful models for you to follow.* They fall into a few basic categories:

- **THE MANTRA MANUAL:** Capture your core values, mindsets, and behaviors in the form of simple, resonant mantras. Aim to keep the total number at fewer than six

---

* For a collection of high-quality culture decks, check out Bretton Putter, "The Very Best Company Culture Decks on the Web," Medium, June 5, 2018, https://medium .com/swlh/the-very-best-company-culture-decks-on-the-web-5a3de60c0bb9.

so that people can remember them. A good example of this is *The Little Book of IDEO,* which consists of a few reflections from the group's leaders, followed by a short chapter on each of their core catchphrases (*Talk Less, Do More; Embrace Ambiguity; Take Ownership; Make Others Successful*), explaining what each mantra means and how best to achieve it.

• **THE YEARBOOK:** In this approach, you fill a book with vibrant images of your people as they put your values into action. This approach works well with large, high-energy cultures; see Zappos for a good example.

• **THE BIOGRAPHY:** Here you take a historical approach, using the story of your group's founding as a way to illustrate and support your core values and identity. This is a useful tool for cultures whose identities are rooted in their unique backstories.

To be sure, you don't need to choose just one. Many groups choose to tell their stories in a number of forms—slide deck, video, book—with each form suited for a particular audience and moment. Don't think of your culture as possessing a single story; rather, think of it as a possessing an ever-growing collection of stories, each reaching your key audiences in a different way. And always be aware that even the most powerful stories get stale over time—so be willing to continually revisit, update, and improve.

"The only thing of real importance
that leaders do is create and manage culture.
If you don't manage culture, it manages you."
—*Edgar Schein*

TIP #60

Build a Model of Excellence

YOUR GROUP'S SKILLS ARE one of its most precious assets. The question is, how do you cultivate and grow those skills, especially in a landscape where many of your people may be working remotely?

One answer is to build a model of excellence: a co-created document that defines and describes the key skills needed to succeed within the organization. A model of excellence functions like a blueprint: It provides a detailed view of what really matters and serves as a template that guides learning and development. Here's how to make yours:

1. Seek out a cross section of people within each role and ask them the following:

   - Name and describe the key skills and strengths that distinguish the top performers in your role from everyone else.
   - Who was the best colleague you ever worked with? Tell a story about what made them special.
   - What are the non-negotiable parts of this job? What do you absolutely need to do well?
   - What's the most useful advice you could give your younger self about succeeding in this job?
   - What parts of this job do people on the outside not see clearly? What is most misunderstood?

2. Capture and define the key skills—no more than ten or so—and list them across the top of a spreadsheet. If appropriate, divide them into domains—like Self, Others, and Organization. Then populate the columns with detailed descriptions of those skills in action, using the quotes gathered in the interviews.

3. Share the model around and create a conversation based on the following questions: What are we missing? What surprises you about this model? How can we use this to create more clarity about the key skills we need?

Don't worry if it's not perfect; this model is not written in stone. The important thing is nurturing a continual conversation about what greatness looks like. If you're like most groups, you'll find that the ensuing conversations end up being their own reward.

BUILDING YOUR GAME PLAN:

STEP FOUR

STRENGTHENING OUR PURPOSE

STRENGTHENING PURPOSE MEANS THINKING like a designer: How can you optimize your group's environment, language, rituals, and structures to funnel energy and attention to what really matters?

Individual Activity #1

CAPTURING YOUR STORY

STORIES ARE THE STRONGEST drug ever invented. They assign value, light up the whole brain, and distill a group's essence into a memorable package.

Write, in simplest outline form, three stories that capture your group at its best. If it helps, follow the problem/breakthrough/benefit structure below.

Story #1:

One day we encountered [NAME THE PROBLEM]

_____

_____

_____

_____

**Everything changed when we
[NAME THE BREAKTHROUGH]**

_____

_____

_____

YOUR TURN

_____

_____

As a result, we created [NAME THE BENEFIT]

_____

_____

_____

Story #2:

One day we encountered [NAME THE PROBLEM]

_____

_____

_____

_____

YOUR TURN

YOUR TURN

Everything changed when we
[NAME THE BREAKTHROUGH]

_____

_____

_____

_____

_____

As a result, we created [NAME THE BENEFIT]

_____

_____

_____

_____

_____

Story #3:

One day we encountered [NAME THE PROBLEM]

_____

_____

Everything changed when we
[NAME THE BREAKTHROUGH]

_____

_____

_____

As a result, we created [NAME THE BENEFIT]

_____

_____

_____

YOUR TURN

Individual Activity #2

QUESTIONS FOR REFLECTION

How might you make your group's sense of purpose more visible, in both the physical and the virtual world?

_____

_____

_____

Name a few events and experiences that have had the biggest positive impact on your group's sense of purpose over the past few years. Why were they impactful?

_____

_____

_____

_____

How often does your group set aside time to pause and reflect together about where you are and where you're headed? How might you do that more often?

_____

_____

_____

_____

YOUR TURN

Group Activity

THIS THIRTY-FIVE-MINUTE ACTIVITY IS designed for groups of four to eight people. Larger groups should divide up accordingly, then share their results with one another.

Materials: Sticky notes, a marker, and a whiteboard (or the digital equivalents)

Have each person select two actions they would like to try from the list. Write the title of each selection on a sticky note and post it on a whiteboard. (five minutes)

YOUR TURN

THE ACTIONS

Embrace Corny Catchphrases

Create a Mantra Map

Do a Best/Barrier Workshop

Start Each Meeting by Linking to Your Group's Purpose

Build the Habit of a Postmeeting Reflection

Share a Weekly Impact Note

Treat Stories as a Precious Resource

Do a Culture Capture

Use Artifacts

Play the Nine Whys Game

Create a Culture Book and/or Deck

Build a Model of Excellence

Or create your own:

1. _____

2. _____

3. _____

1. Ask each person to explain what drew them to these actions and what impact they may have. (ten minutes)

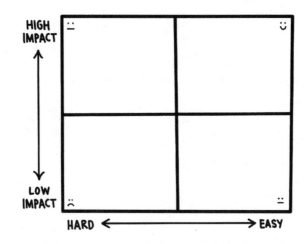

2. As a group, use your collective wisdom to locate each action on the matrix above. The goal is to identify two to three actions that are in the upper-right quadrant: highly impactful and easy to do. (ten minutes)

3. Now that you've chosen your two to three actions, name the specific steps you should take in order to implement these actions. What will you do tomorrow? What tools or materials do you need? Whom should you include in the conversation? (ten minutes)

Action #1 _____

Steps

_____

_____

_____

_____

Action #2 _____

Steps

_____

_____

_____

_____

Action #3 _____

Steps

_____

_____

_____

_____

YOUR TURN

MOVING FORWARD

Just like any other living entity, your group's culture is never fixed; it's continually evolving and changing. To sustain its strength, you need to track your progress and look ahead at the forces that are shaping your landscape. And remember: Not every culture-building action you take will immediately succeed. Think of them as a series of experiments, in which you learn about your group and, just as important, yourself.

Tracking Your Progress

Which culture-building actions did you use? (List them here.)

_____

_____

_____

_____

_____

YOUR TURN

Your turn text appears vertically: YOUR TURN

_____

_____

_____

Which ones were you most excited about?

Action #1:
_____

Action #2:
_____

Action #3:
_____

Did Action #1 work? Why or why not?

_____

_____

_____

If you could do Action #1 over, what might you
and your group do more of? What might you
do differently?

_____

_____

_____

_____

How did you grow as a leader through this?
How did your group grow?

_____

_____

_____

_____

YOUR TURN

YOUR TURN

_____

_____

Did Action #2 work? Why or why not?

_____

_____

_____

_____

If you could do Action #2 over, what might you and your group do more of? What might you do differently?

_____

_____

_____

_____

_____

_____

_____

How did you grow as a leader through this?
How did your group grow?

_____

_____

_____

_____

_____

YOUR TURN

YOUR TURN

Did Action #3 work? Why or why not?

If you could do Action #3 over, what might you and your group do more of? What might you do differently?

_____

_____

_____

How did you grow as a leader through this?
How did your group grow?

_____

_____

_____

_____

_____

_____

_____

YOUR TURN

Looking Ahead

YOUR TURN

> **THOUGHT EXPERIMENT #1:** Imagine you are one year into the future, and your group's culture has improved significantly. What caused that future to happen?

_____

_____

_____

_____

> **THOUGHT EXPERIMENT #2:** Now imagine for a moment that it is one year from now, and your group's culture is significantly worse. What caused that future to happen?

_____

_____

_____

_____

_____

_____

_____

_____

Think about the environment in which your culture
exists and will exist, now and in the next five years or
so. Now name three or four of the major forces that
will affect your group's ability to succeed (for example, speed of change, shifting customer preferences,
increased competition).

_____

_____

_____

_____

YOUR TURN

Now name the handful of group skills you will need
in order to succeed in tomorrow's environment.
For example: Does our group need to be skilled at
innovation? Execution? Building client loyalty?
Name three or four.

_____

_____

_____

_____

Building on that, name the handful of core values
that will support the skill set you just described. It
might be useful to use an If _____, then_____
structure, as in: If we want to be *innovative,* then we
need to value *collaboration.* If we want to build *client
loyalty,* we need to value *relationships.*

_____

_____

_____

_____

_____

_____

YOUR TURN

Write a quick, rough purpose statement for your
future culture: a couple sentences that capture the
impact you want to have in the world and the way in
which you will achieve that impact. Don't worry if it's
not perfect; just get something on paper that you
can share and develop together.

_____

_____

_____

_____

_____

_____

_____

Thanks for reading and engaging. Know that your group's culture, like every culture, is a work in progress. As you move forward, use the following pages to generate ideas, reflect on possibilities, and create conversations.

NOTES AND IDEAS

ACKNOWLEDGMENTS

I'D LIKE TO THANK THE EXTENDED COMMUNITY OF LEADERS, teachers, coaches, scientists, and friends who generously shared their time and expertise. Thanks to my brilliant editor, Andy Ward, and the rest of the Bantam/Penguin Random House team, including Kaeli Subberwal, Chayenne Skeete, Kim Hovey, Elisabeth Magnus, Debbie Aroff, Morgan Hoit, Sarah Breivogel, Richard Elman, Barbara Bachman, Ruby Levesque, and Robert Siek. I'd like to thank my superb agent, David Black, as well as Susan Raihofer, Rachel Ludwig, Anagha Putrevu, and Ayla Zuraw-Friedland. Thanks to everyone at the Cleveland Guardians for their warmth, smarts, and generosity, and thanks to fellow short kings Paul Cox and Doug Vahey. I'd like to thank my brothers, Maurice and Jon Coyle, and my niece Rosie Coyle, for their thoughtful help. I'm grateful to my kids, Aidan, Katie, Lia, and Zoe, for their insights and inspiration—and for the collaborative delight that Zoe provided by helping to brainstorm and build the illustrations in this book. Most of all, I'd like to thank my wife, Jenny, whose love, wisdom, and support make all good things happen.

ABOUT THE AUTHOR

DANIEL COYLE is the *New York Times* bestselling author of *The Culture Code, The Talent Code, The Little Book of Talent, The Secret Race, Lance Armstrong's War,* and *Hardball: A Season in the Projects.* Coyle, who works as a special advisor to the Cleveland Guardians, lives in Cleveland, Ohio, during the school year and in Homer, Alaska, during the summer with his wife, Jenny, and their four children.

danielcoyle.com

Twitter: @DanielCoyle

This book was set in Fournier, a typeface named for Pierre-Simon Fournier (1712–68), the youngest son of a French printing family. He started out engraving woodblocks and large capitals, then moved on to fonts of type. In 1736 he began his own foundry and made several important contributions in the field of type design; he is said to have cut 147 alphabets of his own creation. Fournier is probably best remembered as the designer of St. Augustine Ordinaire, a face that served as the model for the Monotype Corporation's Fournier, which was released in 1925.